A Country Boy's Walk with God!

Inspired by God, Written by Allen C. Laws

Dedication:

First and foremost, I dedicate this book to our awesome God Who by His grace and through His Holy Spirit gave me the inspiration to write these stories.

Lord Jesus, what You have done to rescue and redeem sinners like me is an immeasurable sacrifice worthy of all praise.

Thank You sweet Holy Spirit for guiding my thoughts and words throughout this entire endeavor. Because of all each of you have done and continue to do in my life, my days are filled with joyful expectation, hope, confidence and love. To God be all the glory!

Contents

ABOUT THE AUTHOR

Allen Laws – Allen was born in Kansas City, Missouri in 1962. He was then raised in central Iowa until the age of 14. At that time his parents moved the entire family to southern Arkansas where he lived until 1980. Allen then moved to Texas where he married the love of his life, Karen. They have two grown children, Jody and Allen Jr., and to date have five grandchildren. Until they found The FORT Discipleship Center in Tomball, TX, Allen acknowledges he was lost, bouncing from church to church searching for something he and Karen had been unable to find. Allen is currently studying to soon become a licensed lay minister at The FORT Discipleship Center. 'Thank God for the path he has put me on.'

If for any reason you would like to contact me, about my book or your walk with God, I would love to hear from you.

Please feel free to email me at axlaws@yahoo.com

Preface

In the following pages I have documented a few of the specific times, events, circumstances, emotions, victories and miserable failures that have occurred throughout my life's journey. I have purposefully chosen to be open and transparent in sharing some of my triumphs as well as tragedies hoping to personally connect with each of you who honor me by taking time to read my story. My prayer is that each of these short stories from my life will inspire you to Hope for the future and a steadfast confidence that the days ahead will be better than all the days of your past in Jesus' name. I make no claims to be any great saint, but I am a grateful recipient and witness of God's grace and greatness. Therefore, I am certainly one who can testify that no matter what this life throws at you, our mighty God will faithfully cover, protect and keep you in His love.

My one challenge to every Christian who might read my story is, 'Make certain you understand and take heed that satan (never capitalized in my writings, he doesn't deserve that respect) and his minions are always on the prowl searching for the unsuspecting and naïve to steal, kill and destroy everything within their lives *(John 10:10) The thief's purpose is to steal and kill and destroy. My purpose is to give them a rich and satisfying life.*

Thank you for choosing to read this book. I sincerely pray these stories will motivate you to change wherever change is needed, then finish strong for the glory of our mighty God. The enemy is cunning and tireless in his scheming continually seeking to bring you to the place of despair, confusion, apathy and ultimate condemnation. If I can learn to walk in victory in Christ, then ANY ONE CAN!

Acknowledgments

I would be remiss if I didn't take a moment to acknowledge and honor a few of the people the Lord has mercifully placed in my life to help me with my walk of faith in the Lord Jesus. First, I want to thank my amazing wife, Karen. Without your love and support throughout all these years I sincerely do not believe I would have ever come to know Jesus as my personal Lord and Savior. I love you. Thank you to each of my children for never abandoning me, even though there were many times you would have been justified in doing so. I love you. Thank you to my pastors Jerry and Donna Williams for your patience, guidance and consistent love for me and my family.

I would also like to thank Mike Irvin for his kindness in giving me permission to use his artwork for the cover of my book. Mike is an awesome artist, who's work is inspirational to me. If you are ever in or near Clifton, Texas, stop in and have a look at his work.

Lastly, thank you to all of you who believed in me even though I had little or no belief in myself. I thank God for each and every one of you.

(All Scripture references have been taken from the NLT.)

Chapter One
My Walk with God!

Ecclesiastes 1:13-14 I devoted myself to search for understanding and to explore by wisdom everything being done under heaven. I soon discovered that God has dealt a tragic existence to the human race. 14 I observed everything going on under the sun, and really, it is all meaningless—like chasing the wind.

Oh, how I wish I could begin this book by telling you that I have consistently proven to be a God-chaser, but that just isn't the truth. Through the years my personal walk with God would probably best be described as 'up and down', much like you would envision a see-saw on the playground going up and down. Yet, amazingly the Lord has continually pursued me and proven His love for me by giving me many undeniable demonstrations of His power and presence along the way. One such demonstration occurred approximately twenty years ago when I was attending a small church where my brother-in-law was recognized as one of the pastoral staff. On my third visit I was unexpectedly overwhelmed by the manifest presence of God. Suddenly, even though my eyes were closed, all I could see was a brilliant vision of Jesus. I spontaneously raised my hands in praise to Him as the eyes of my heart were illuminated and I SAW THE LORD! He was standing in His robe and sandaled feet surrounded by the vibrant Light I had first seen. Then I heard a Voice speaking directly to me saying, KNEEL BEFORE ME! The Voice was so real my immediate thought was someone in the church was playing a joke on me. So, with that thought in mind I quickly opened my eyes expecting to catch the jokester in the act. Instead, all I saw were the women and children close to me, but no man was anywhere near me. In that instant I knew it was the Voice of God speaking directly to me. I grabbed my wife's hand and without hesitation made my way to the altar and obediently knelt down as I had been commanded. In the next few moments, the presence of God filled my body, soul and spirit with inexpressible love and grace. It was the most awesome and indescribable feeling I had ever known.

I returned the next Sunday filled with expectation of what God might do with me again. Surprisingly, a young man I had never met approached me sharing he was scheduled for surgery the next week. He then asked me if I would have the church body pray for him. It was the custom of this church to pray for everyone at the end of the service, so when that time came, I went forward on behalf of this young man and requested prayer for him. One of the pastors heard my request and said, 'We pray for him every week, so we don't need to do it again today'. I was not expecting that kind of response, especially from one of the pastors, and fired back an immediate response, 'You don't have to pray for him, but I will'. By the grace of God, I heard a few days later that the young man didn't have to undergo surgery after all. Hallelujah! The sad ending to all this is the little church in which I had so powerfully experienced the presence of God disbanded only a few weeks later due to an inability of the leaders to come into agreement. Pride always goes before a fall.

After that I only attended church sporadically at best. Each time I would visit some other church I would wait to see if the presence of God would manifest like that time in the little church where I had the vision of Jesus. Time after time I visited church after church, but when I didn't sense the presence of God, I wouldn't go back. That all changed in February of 2011. My brother-in-law and sister-in-law invited her sister and me to their new church. Getting with the extended family was at best uncomfortable for me, so I declined their first few invitations. It wasn't long before my sister-in-law convinced me that I had to meet the pastor who had a different outlook, totally different attitude, and was really easy to talk with. So, after a year of persistence from my sister-in-law, I finally relented and headed to the service the next Sunday. The FORT Discipleship Center at that time was meeting in a hotel conference room. To my dismay though the preacher that was supposed to be my "kindred spirit" wasn't preaching, it was my brother-in-law. Even though I was disappointed to find out that "Jerry" wasn't there due to other obligations he had to attend to, the whole experience of our first visit was very pleasant. So, we decided to go back the next week. That second visit is when my kindred spirit was there preaching. My wife and I entered the conference room during worship, late as usual. We found seats on the back row. When the worship finished, we sat down. The first person to speak was a lady who was testifying about a child in her classroom who was being tormented with wickedness. As she poured out her heart for this child, my legs began to literally tremble, there was nothing I could to stop the shaking. I asked my wife for some paper and a pen as I felt compelled to write down some of the things this lady had revealed were tormenting the child. Once the lady was done speaking and they had prayed for this child, pastor Jerry then began his message for that day, that's when everything changed in our lives for good.

During the message I laid my head down quietly praying asking the Lord for some kind of a sign. I did this because I had become overwhelmed with an ever-intensifying feeling that I had to get up and address the congregation, but I was a visitor. The longer I waited the stronger the burden became. That's when I asked the Lord for a very specific sign, 'God, if this is really You, then have pastor Jerry call out my name in the middle of his message', a pastor I had never met or spoken with. Moments later unbelievably pastor Jerry called out my name, but when he did so he also included several other names of those in attendance. That should have been enough for me, but it wasn't. That's why I know God has a sense of humor. I bowed my head and prayed again, 'Lord, if this is really You, then have pastor Jerry call out ONLY my name and no one else's'. I don't think pastor Jerry even took a breath between the time I had finished my prayer when he CALLED OUT ONLY MY NAME! I immediately leaned over to my wife and shocked her by saying, 'I have to speak to the congregation'. I had never done anything like this before, so you can imagine the look of astonishment on the face of my wife as I stood up in the middle of pastor Jerry's message. If Jerry had actually known me, he would have thought I was leaving, but I walked directly over to one of the elders and expressed that the Lord had given me something to say to the congregation. Since pastor Jerry was still speaking, the elder asked if I wanted him to interrupt the message. I told him, 'Oh no, but I just don't want anyone to leave before I can share what the Lord has placed on my heart'. As soon as pastor Jerry finished his message, leaning on his music stand, he turned his head and spoke directly to me, 'Allen, I believe you have something to share'. My legs felt like I was walking on rubber. He then motioned for me to come forward and address the people. All I could say was, 'God has something He wants me to share with everyone'. Pastor Jerry was smiling from ear to ear and encouraged me to say whatever was on my heart. I first said, 'I really don't know what to say'. Then someone from the congregation said, 'Say what's on your heart, brother'. I then took out the notes I had written down concerning the child being tormented by satan. Then a boldness came upon me as I said, 'The Lord wants us to pray for this little girl as a group'. Pastor Jerry handed me the microphone, placed his arm over my shoulders, then said, 'Allen, go ahead and lead us in prayer for this little girl'. I sheepishly responded, 'I don't know how' to which pastor Jerry said, 'Just speak to God'.

What happened in the next few moments was AWESOME! And, by the way, the little girl is doing much, much better today. Hallelujah!

Thank You, Lord, for putting people in my life who love You and are guided by Your Holy Spirit. Thank You for my family, and my extended church family. Thank You for giving me the opportunity to reach others for Your Kingdom and Your glory. Oh Lord, I pray that with Your help, guidance and wisdom I can reach those who would have never had the opportunity to know You as their Lord. In Jesus name I pray.

Chapter Two
Running!

1 Timothy 1:16 But God had mercy on me so that Christ Jesus could use me as a prime example of His great patience with even the worst sinners. Then others will realize that they, too, can believe in Him and receive eternal life.

I don't think it would be too much of a stretch to say that from our earliest childhood days until that moment we each take our final breath; our lives are continually bombarded with all sorts of distractions that more often than not tend to limit rather than enhance our involvement with God. I know in my case, as an impressionable child, I grew up in a home that wasn't focused or centered on God, much less guided by Him. Still, I have many wonderful childhood memories of loving parents who gave me everything I basically wanted and were always there faithfully supporting all my school and sports events. The only thing I can honestly say they didn't provide was a home that honored or worshipped the Lord. As a matter of fact, I never even knew my parents possessed any belief in God until I was already a young adult. That doesn't mean that God wasn't ever a topic of discussion in our conversations, because He was. However, never did those discussions include any dialog about Jesus Christ and our desperate need to believe in Him as our Lord and Savior. It's easy now to look back and see how so many little things distracted and even dictated the direction my life took when I was younger. Looking back, it's almost as if everything I was doing in actuality hindered me from finding, much less following Christ as my Savior and Lord. Wow! It's hard to think that so many of those distractions actually aided me in 'running away' from the Lord rather than running to Him. How wonderful today to be able to see how Jesus has been faithfully 'running after' me all the days of my life. Thank You, *For the Son of Man, came to 'seek and to save' those who are lost. (Luke 19:10).*

I was thirteen when I first started having serious thoughts about the Lord, which resulted in my deciding to become part of a local youth group. My parents had no idea what was going on, but in those days, I was looking for something to help make sense of all the emotional ups and downs brought on by exploding hormones causing me (and every other teenager) to be ultra-sensitive about anything and everything. Somehow, I just felt that finding the answers had something to do with finding the Lord. Strange as it may sound, the real reason I joined the youth group was to find out about the God I didn't yet know, and just assumed joining a 'Christian' youth group would give me the answers I was so desperately seeking. Instead, the young female leader of the youth group took me aside and began teaching me things far different than what I was seeking. In just a few weeks our little 'fling' was over, and I dejectedly left the youth group still having no understanding of what it meant to 'know' Jesus personally. Consequently, I fell back into what I knew and understood retreating into the safety zone of doing everything that caused me to 'run away' from the Lord, even though that's not what I wanted to be doing.

Seven years later, at the age of twenty, my soon to be wife and I were invited to a family prayer meeting at her grandmother's house. I remember how much I wanted to fit in with the people attending. The truth is what I really wanted was the one thing I believed they had that I had been looking for the past seven years, a relationship with the Lord. As the night went on, I did everything I could to imitate their actions – hands in the air, praying aloud in the presence of others (this was my first time to do many of these things). At one point the 'family' all gathered around me and began encouraging me to speak in tongues. They kept telling me, 'Just let the words roll off your tongue'. I was doing everything I knew to do to follow their instructions, but then I heard one of my soon to be wife's cousins say, 'He doesn't know what he is doing'. The moment I heard those words I began to withdraw from everything that was going on, then only a few moments later I turned and told my fiancé (who had not heard the words her cousin said) it was time for us to leave. It was already getting late, so she agreed and we left soon after. As we left, I chose not to say anything about what I had heard knowing it would have upset her to the point she would have confronted her cousin to make sure he 'got his heart right'. All I kept thinking was, 'Here I am again, letting others dictate what actions I should take to find God, then have an active and personal relationship with Him in my life. Consequently, I did what I had always done and ran back into the safety of my life of sin and separation from God.

For the next thirty years I settled into a lifestyle of wandering about this world completely lost, oblivious to God's purpose and plan for my life, and to be honest just simply didn't care anymore. The great News is God still cared and was all the while working behind the scenes of my pitiful life making certain there would be multiple opportunities for me to see, hear and respond to His TRUTH. What I eventually realized is that God is the same yesterday, today and forever, and His promise to never leave or forsake me was always in place, and He was always just a prayer away. What tremendous joy it was to my heart to find out later that God was always there protecting and quietly calling me even through all the years I didn't willingly choose to have Him as part of my life. Although I wrestle with thoughts of how different my life would be today had I just answered His call years earlier, I still am forever grateful that the 'day' came when I sincerely repented of my sinful ways and accepted Jesus as my Master, Lord, Savior and King. I can never get back the lost and wasted years, but I can rest in His promise that the 'years the locust has eaten, I will restore' (Joel 2:25).

Dear Father God, thank You for being my Savior. Forgive me for allowing others in my life to push me in a direction I know leads me away from You. I pray these stories from my life will first bring You glory, and also help others to find You much earlier in this momentary life. May all those who choose to read these snapshots of my life be inspired to walk with You in an ever-growing intimacy, daily seeking and finding You and the joy that comes from being in Your presence. In Jesus name I pray.

Chapter Three
Grace!

Jeremiah 29:11 For I know the plans I have for you," says the LORD. "They are plans for good and not for disaster, to give you a future and a hope.

There is a three-letter word in this scripture that I want to focus on for a moment. The three-letter word that jumped out to me was the word 'you'. Every time I read this passage I never feel as though God is singling out the Jews, or the wealthy of that day. Neither do I sense He is trying to lure the scholars into a spiritual debate or is focused simply on 'good people'. The Word of God has always been straight forward and basically easy to understand to me because I never try to see hidden messages between the lines. It's right there in front of our eyes for all to see, hear and plainly understand, if they just will read it with an open heart. I love the fact that my awesome God is so direct and plain spoken. That's why I believe in this passage the word 'you' relates to all of us, no matter what our background or ethnicity. He has plans for

'YOU' if 'you' will choose to love Him and believe upon His Son, our Savior, Jesus Christ.

I love God with all my heart, but I have to be honest and say there are far too many times I get really frustrated at just how easily I (and so many others I know who sincerely love the Lord) become discouraged and allow doubt and a smothering sense of insecurity to creep into our thoughts. How I long for the day I can consistently make every discouraging thought come into submission to Jesus. Simply writing down those words reminds me of one of our elders, Randy, who always says, 'It's all about Jesus'. He was recently teaching at church bringing an informative and very thought-provoking lesson. Before he finished the question was asked, 'How long have you been waiting for what you now see God doing at church?' Some of the answers I heard were, 'All my life', 'for more than forty years', 'thirty years'. I sat there hoping no one would ask me that question because I was embarrassed to acknowledge that most of my adult life, I've run FROM God rather than run TO or FOR God. Suddenly my mind was going crazy as

I began telling myself, 'You don't have any right or business standing up in front of these people who have faithfully been in church and waiting on God for so long'. While my mind was playing havoc with my heart, suddenly I heard these words in my spirit, 'I have a plan for you'. At that moment a smile came on my face which pastor Jerry immediately saw. Hallelujah! In the next few moments, I began pondering whether or not anyone can ever truly realize the immensity of the grace God has given us, unless they have a personal encounter with the Lord and the TRUTH found in His Word. I concluded in my mind that I don't believe it's possible to possess any real understanding of the measure of God's grace without studying, believing and obeying the Word of God. God has a 'plan' and 'purpose' for every person on the planet, no matter whether they ever 'see' it, 'know' it, 'find' it or even 'seek' it. The plan will always be there, and that's part of the power and glory of God's grace. Wow!

Several years ago, we were on a family trip to Kansas to visit our relatives there. The entire trip was a little odd from the outset as we were driving three vehicles. My brother and his family were in the lead in their vehicle, while my daughter and I were in the middle driving my sister's van that we had borrowed for a short time. My wife and newborn son were bringing up the rear in our car. It was truly a family caravan, and is the only time in our 35 years of marriage we've ever taken two vehicles on vacation just for our family.

We began the journey with my four-year-old daughter riding with me in the van while my wife had the pleasure of traveling with our son. The twelve-hour trek started out just the way you would hope for, smoothly and uneventful. Again, my brother and his family were in front, I was in the middle and Karen brought up the end of the small caravan. Not too long after starting I remember stopping in McAlester, Oklahoma just a few miles before the Indian Nation Turnpike. We grabbed some lunch, stretched our legs and then we were off again.

Soon after leaving McAlester we entered Turnpike. Even though this route has tolls, we always take it because the road is in pretty good shape. At the time, it had a speed limit of 75 on it, so we all know what that means, within moments we were traveling 85-90 mph on the highway. We had only been on the turnpike for a short time when I noticed behind me that Karen was weaving back and forth from the outside lane to the shoulder. Since this was long before cell phones, I couldn't call her to find out what was going on. We were probably no more than 10-miles into the turnpike when I finally had seen enough of my wife and son weaving all over the highway. I quickly found what I considered a safe place to pull over so we could all park on the shoulder. I told Jody (the four-year-old) to stay in the van, that I would be right back after checking on her mommy. Thankfully Karen saw me pulling over and pulled in dutifully right behind me on the highway. As I approached her vehicle, I am confident she could see I was worried and upset about something by the look on my face. The truth is I've never been able to easily mask or hide my emotions from anyone, much less the ones I love. While walking up to her car I motioned for her to "roll" her window down. I then asked, 'What's going on? You are swerving back and forth all over the freeway!" She smiled at me, and then told me she was just playing with our newborn tickling his toes and goo-gooing him. I have to be honest and admit that in that moment I went ballistic. While standing on the side of the Indian Nation Turnpike I became very, very animated causing people that were driving by to slow down to see what was going on. I finally asked Karen, "What do you think would happen if you were to crest a hill, you can't see over and you've wandered onto the shoulder driving a Lincoln Mercury Tracer at a speed of 75 mph or greater and there's a stranded vehicle on the shoulder?" She looked at me with a very shocked look on her face and said, "Oh my goodness, thank you, I never thought about anything like that happening." She said she was sorry and assured me she would pay more attention to her driving.

After calming down, I got back into my vehicle and we all got back on the freeway. Amazingly, as we came over the next hill there on the shoulder set a full-size van broken down. Thank You, Jesus for stopping us before going over that hill.

So, you see, I believe God not only knows the plans He has for us, but He is mercifully there for people that aren't currently living the life He has set into motion for us. Even though we don't know what the future holds, He knows it all and is at work in our lives preparing us for what lies ahead.

Dear Father God, keep us safe in our travels wherever they may take us, whether it is a short trip in our neighborhood, or a trip across our beautiful country.
Father keep those that are lost safe from harm and give them the chance to find the Love You have for them. I pray You would continue to give the lost many opportunities to one day live for You that they, too, might find and acknowledge the amazing plan You've put in place for their lives. In Jesus name I pray.

Chapter Four
Pride

Isaiah 2:11 Human pride will be brought down, and human arrogance will be humbled. Only the Lord will be exalted on that Day of Judgment.

Note: In this short story I have included more scriptures than usual simply due to the gravity of living so many years of my life full of pride and arrogance.

Honestly, it was only recently the Lord began to stir in my heart the need to speak out on this difficult and delicate subject. Who am I to talk to anyone else about 'pride' in their lives? Yet, here I am feeling compelled to address this topic even though I spent years not fully understanding the true meaning of pride and just how deadly it is if allowed to go unchallenged in our daily lives.

My thoughts on this subject begins on Sunday evening of January 6th, 2013. I remember vividly how that particular night something happened that caused me to feel greatly disrespected. I immediately confronted the person who (in my mind) had maligned my character only to get a barrage of double talk in return. That infuriated me even more unleashing even more anger in my heart until I almost reached a boiling point. Although I held it together in front of the person who had maligned me, my emotions were much like a freight train going downhill without any brakes – headed straight for a horrible wreck. I later blew up in front of my wife who amazingly handled the situation much better than I did. I thought later how I kept hitting her with angry words much like a professional boxer would hit a punching bag. She patiently took all my 'punches' until I was done, then she took some anxiety medicine to help her recover.

The next morning (Monday – 1/07/13) I woke up still angry, and of all things, late for work. I quickly got ready and rushed out of the house. To make matters even worse, on my way to work, I realized I had forgotten several things I really needed for work. I decided to go on to work anyway, and if possible, would swing back by the house later that day to pick those things up. Things worked out for me to stop back by the house around lunchtime. My wife, Karen, was really surprised to see me walk in, but could immediately tell I was still angry and in a terrible mood because of what had happened the night before. Being the amazing wife, she is she quickly and quietly fixed me a sack lunch leaving me to continue sulking in my anger. As soon as she was done, I kissed her goodbye and returned to my job. My responsibilities at work required that I spend a lot of time driving from one site to another. It was always my custom while driving around the great Houston area to listen to one of our local Christian radio stations, KSBJ. I usually found that listening to Christian music throughout the day helped to keep my mind and heart in touch with the Lord.

On this day, however, I chose NOT to listen to Christian music, but rather to turn the radio to a local sports station convincing myself I was doing this to find out the latest news on the Houston Texans. I soon reached my first jobsite, then parked and turned off my truck. As I checked out the jobsite and began filling out the necessary paperwork for the crew, the Holy Spirit ambushed my mind flooding my thoughts with the lyrics of a song I had heard on a different day listening to Christian music. In my mind I immediately said, 'Not today God', then quickly jumped back into my truck and cranked up the sports drowning out everything else. I finished the rest of my day listening to local sports rather than KSBJ whose station slogan is 'God Listens'.

The punch line to this story is I learned that day that God really does listen, and He is always there. I later realized how the Holy Spirit was trying to get my attention and help lead me out of the 'funk' I had allowed myself to get in, a 'funk' that lasted for days all because I got upset over something someone said about me. Then I thought about how the Holy Spirit rode around with me all that day and how I tried to drown out His Voice with sports news blaring inside the cab of the truck. Amazingly, He just left me to simmer and wallow in my own self-pity and pride.

I finally sat down with my wife and shared all this with her telling her how I felt totally unworthy to ever speak again in our church. (Our pastor would often ask me to address the congregation and share many of my life-stories with the people showing God's mercy, forgiveness, love and power.) As she pondered what to say, she came over and put her arms around me, then said, 'You need to open the line back up with the Lord and continue to be obedient'. That was truly a 'word' from the Lord as I felt the anger, self-pity and pride leave almost instantly. As soon as the anger was gone, I was filled with remorse and shame over how I had treated the Lord. I didn't choose to praise Him or even speak to Him for over twenty-four hours, but instead let my pride separate me from fellowshipping with my Lord and Savior, Jesus Christ.

I pray this example from my life in some small way helps some of you choose to willingly and immediately let go of any pride or anger that is keeping you separated and out of fellowship with the Lord. Nothing anyone says or does to us is more important than hearing the Voice of God every day and staying in communion with Him.

1 Samuel 17:28 But when David's oldest brother, Eliab, heard David talking to the men, he was angry. 'What are you doing around here anyway?', he demanded. 'What about those few sheep you're supposed to be taking care of? I know about your pride and deceit. You just want to see the battle!'

Job 35:12 And when they cry out, God does not answer because of their pride.

Job 36:9 He shows them the reason. He shows them their sins of pride.

Psalms 73:6 They wear pride like a jeweled necklace and clothe themselves with cruelty.

Psalms 76:12 For He breaks the pride of princes, and the kings of the earth fear Him.

Proverbs 6:3 Follow my advice and save yourself, for you have placed yourself at your friend's mercy. Now swallow your pride; go and beg to have your name erased.

Proverbs 11:2 Pride leads to disgrace, but with humility comes wisdom.

Proverbs 29:23 Pride ends in humiliation, while humility brings honor.

Jeremiah 13:15 Listen and pay attention! Do not be arrogant, for the Lord has spoken.

Prov 16:18 Pride goes before destruction, and haughtiness before a fall.

ACCEPTABLE PRIDE:

Philippians 1:26 And when I come to you again, you will have even more reason to take pride in Christ Jesus because of what He is doing through me.

Thank You, Lord for mercifully allowing me the privilege and continued opportunity to follow You. Thank You for leading me down a path wherein I learn valuable lessons that You are using to lay a strong and firm foundation to my faith, a faith that You planted in my heart that I might one day love and obey You. Help me, Lord, to live each moment of each day in fellowship with You doing only those things that benefit Your purpose in my life and bring honor to You. In Jesus name I pray.

Chapter Five
Alone

1 Peter 2:11 Dear friends, I warn you as 'temporary residents and foreigners' to keep away from worldly desires that wage war against your very souls.

I've never really been what you would call a 'people person', but have always been more of a home body preferring to hang around the house with the family or by myself. I've always had the idea that if I couldn't do whatever needed done by myself or with the help of my family, then it wasn't that important. When I became born-again that kind of thinking remained with me as I thought if God and 'me' couldn't take care of whatever the problem might be, then I would just live with the problem until 'we' figured it out. Well, I WAS WRONG!

Thankfully, I've come to realize and truly understand this kind of thinking and behavior is in direct opposition to the way God intends us to live our daily lives for

Him and His glory. Trying to manage my walk with God alone was not only ignorant and a huge mistake, but it led me down several slippery and treacherous paths God never intended me to be on. Here's what I now know and live by: you cannot 'fight the good fight of faith' alone. In short, attempting to 'fight the good fight of faith' alone is like getting into the boxing ring with Mike Tyson with one hand tied behind your back. Now that's just plain stupid.

I'm beginning to understand even more why the Lord gives us the command,

Hebrews 10:24-25 Let us consider how to stimulate one another to love and good deeds, 25. not forsaking our own assembling together, as is the habit of some, but encouraging one another; and all the more as you see the day drawing near.

Going to church is never an option with God, but too often was nothing more than an optional convenience in my mind. Church isn't just important to my life, it is vital. My pastor describes church as a place full of 'body parts'. He often explains that what gives a 'body part' such great value it not simply the 'body part' separated out and alone, but what that particular 'body part' gives to the other 'body parts' it is connected with. For instance, a finger has little value unless it is connected to a hand. The hand has little value and soon dies unless it is connected to the arm. That means each one of us have amazing value when we are 'connected together' and growing as God intended. It's truly an amazing experience to have like-minded people in your life, people you love, trust and can count on when in need.

Never forget satan has come to 'steal, kill and destroy' our lives. He is a master hunter and knows the easiest way to take us out is to get us separated from the pack (the church body of like-minded brothers and sisters). He will stop at nothing to convince you it is a 'good thing' to be alone. Once you believe that lie, then he has you in his crosshairs and will soon attack.

How often have we all witnessed satan separating and dividing Christians who only days earlier were telling each other they loved one another? Anytime you see Christians separating from other Christians you can know for certain satan is hunting in that specific flock of sheep. One by one he will carefully separate the weak ones from the stronger and then 'take them out'. I, for one, am tired of seeing that happen over and over and have committed the rest of my life to staying connected and never again find myself ALONE and doing things on my own.

If we were to all be honest, we would have to admit we've all been separated out and 'taken out' by satan too many times in the past. I, for one, do not ever want to be 'taken out' by him again. By God's grace and in Jesus' name I am determined to never choose to be ALONE (separated out) again, but will work to be that faithful and effective 'body part' who helps to give value and purpose to other 'body parts'. The goal is to connect enough 'body parts' together to make up a whole 'BODY', the BODY of

Christ. When that happens, and each part is working properly, then Jesus will be lifted up and ALL men will see Him and be drawn to Him as their Savior.

So, let me ask you, do you want to be a faithful, functioning and valuable 'body part' for the Lord giving life, value and purpose to other possibly weaker 'body parts'? Or, do you want to continue in your stubborn ignorance all ALONE allowing satan to keep you depressed, ashamed, ineffective and unproductive in your walk with God?

Far too long I lived ALONE which resulted in my having no control over my thoughts or actions. My mind was corrupted, my heart was corrupted, and my walk with God was at best weak and anemic. Those who live like this all have one thing in common – they live everyday of their lives with hidden, unconquered sin. If that is where you are today, then do what you must do to be healed and delivered:

James 5:13-16 Is anyone among you suffering? Then he must pray. Is anyone cheerful? He is to sing praises. 14 Is anyone among you sick? Then he must call for the elders of the church and they are to pray over him, anointing him with oil in the name of the Lord; 15 and the prayer offered in faith will restore the one who is sick, and the Lord will raise him up, and if he has committed sins, they will be forgiven him. 16 Therefore, confess your sins to one another, and pray for one another so that you may be healed.

My heavenly Father, I pray You would give me a keen awareness of Your blessed Holy Spirit Who lives within me ready to awaken my heart and mind every day to Your purpose, power and will for my life. Oh, how I pray You would help me to be a faithful conduit of Your love to others. On those days I feel isolated from Your and Your presence do not let me aimlessly wander about all alone, but rather draw me quickly back to that place of safety and surety with those who call upon Your name from a pure heart. Apart from You I can do

nothing, I am nothing! In You I find
Strength to face every danger and every day
with hope, confidence and a living
expectation that the days ahead will be
better than the days behind. I pray You
would bring me to the place where my life is
useful in Your hands to help strengthen
others who may be weaker and in danger of
being 'taken out' by the enemy of our souls.
Thank You for Your mercy, grace, love,
power and presence that are ever working in
me and changing me to be more and more
like Jesus, in Whose Name I pray!

Chapter Six
Debt

Romans 3:23 *For everyone has sinned; we all fall short of God's glorious standard.*

Throughout my life I have often heard people say that I view things from a different perspective than most other people they know. Since becoming a Christian, I've come to understand this is the way God created me, but also one of the specific ways He chooses to speak to my heart. Consequently, when I began hearing Him speak to my heart concerning 'debt', I had to take a few moments and pause wondering where this all might lead. Discussing what people do with their money is at the very least a delicate subject that if not handled carefully can even lead to volatile disagreement between friends and family. Remarkably, I've seen this topic strike fear in the heart of even the strongest of leaders in the Church. Nevertheless, it's something the Lord has been speaking to my heart about, so I must be faithful to share what I believe the Lord has spoken to my heart.

Let me begin by asking the question, 'Is there anyone you know who can truly say they are debt free?' The most obvious debt most people live with is what they owe the banks and credit card companies. There are other kinds of 'debts' we owe that are not financial such as being indebted to those who do 'good' to us on a daily basis. These types of 'debt' usually compels us to endeavor to 'pay back' the 'good deed' done to us by doing a 'good deed' for another. All that is good and understandable, but THE GREATEST DEBT WE OWE is one most people rarely or never consider…and that is the incomparable DEBT we ALL OWE Jesus Christ for coming to rescue, save, redeem and deliver us from the bondage of sin. That DEBT alone is why I don't believe anyone could ever truly say they are 'debt free' or ever will be for that matter.

Whenever I think of being 'debt free' I usually associate that term with those who have either won the lottery, paid off their home, paid off their cars, paid off their student loans or paid off any other loans they may have acquired. To take it another step further, these people then live their lives paying cash for everything having eliminated even using a credit card. But is that really 'debt free'? I still don't think so! With the way society now functions it would be extremely difficult and unusual for anyone to ever really have the opportunity to proclaim, 'I am debt free'.

My wife and I are currently praying about (and trying) to purchase a home. We are really trusting the Lord this will be our last home, one that is God's choice for us that we will use for His glory. We long to have our own home dedicated to the Lord and filled with His presence, anointing and power. We fully realize that unless the Lord is in the center of choosing and blessing this home, then it will be nothing more than a building with walls where only emptiness and sorrow will remain. However, when He chooses the right home for us, then we are certain it will be resonating with His blessed

Holy Spirit, with the joy of His presence and the joy of our salvation. It will be a place wherein we hear His voice, receive His guidance and are filled with His wisdom as we daily search the Scriptures and seek His face. Once again, that will be a 'debt' we can never repay and will gladly always owe…a debt of gratitude and praise.

As I continued pondering this topic, I was moved to tears realizing that no matter what happens in this life (good or bad), I can never be 'debt free' because of all the Lord has done for me through Christ! So, let me ask you the question again, 'Do you believe there is any possibility you might one day ever be truly debt free?' Personally, I know I will never be able to repay the debt I owe for God's grace, mercy, love, kindness, forgiveness and salvation in Christ. I am a grateful 'debtor' for all the Lord Jesus has done and continues to do in my life and family.

As for me and my house we have committed our lives and our future to living according to God's commands and 'do' what is right every day. We understand our efforts will never be enough to reduce the amount of gratitude we owe the Lord Jesus Christ, but we don't see our effort as any kind of 'payback', but rather as an amazing 'privilege'. Now every day we expectantly seek the Lord's guidance, forgiveness, mercy, grace and truth knowing that whatever we ask that's in accordance to His will and His Word He will provide abundantly. What a life! What a Lord! What a Savior Who poured out His sinless blood and gave His Life that we might have Life, and that Life more abundantly. Now that's a debt I will joyfully live with the rest of my life. Forever indebted to Christ while forever debt free from sin in Christ.

In closing, let me ask: Have you received Christ as your Savior and become an eternal 'debtor' to Christ for cleansing you of all your sin? Have you committed your entire life to the Lord understanding it's the least you can do to honor His sacrifice for your sin? Are you seeking to live according to His commands? If your answer to any of the above questions is 'no', then at this very moment call out to Jesus and be gloriously saved forever becoming indebted to His mercy and forgiveness.

My dear heavenly Father, I know all too well how I daily fall short of Your purpose and plans for my life. I know I am still helplessly weak and desperately in need of Your truth, guidance, love, anointing and presence. Help me, O my God, to walk more and more consistently in Your righteousness fully submitted to Your commands in my heart and soul. Enable me to be a faithful witness that I might see many of those I meet come to know Jesus as their Lord and Savior. Oh, how I long to be more like You bringing You more and more honor and glory through my words and actions. I pray this in Jesus' mighty name.

Chapter Seven
Discipline

Hebrews 12:11 All discipline for the moment seems not to be joyful, but sorrowful; yet to those who have been trained by it, afterwards it yields the peaceful fruit of righteousness.

There are very few people other than my wife that know I am the youngest of seven in my family. I have four half-brothers, one half-sister and one full blood sister. Although technically I call them my half-brothers and half-sister, but my half-brother, Ron, has stood by me my entire life. He was the only one of the six I actually grew up around as the other half-brothers, half-sister and full blood sister were either already moved out or living in another part of the country with their mother. Consequently, my older half-brother Ron was always there no matter what I was going through or what I had done. That's why I never imagined it could be possible to have a better brother. Ron and I both grew up in a home with parents that were older than most of the parents of the other kids our age in school. Most of our friends thought of us as being 'well off' even though our parents weren't wealthy by any means. Even so, I can't remember any time we ever really 'wanted' for anything in our home. So, growing up in a home where money was never any real issue, my parents were older and I was the 'baby' of the family (the youngest of all seven children), I guess there is no other way to say this but, 'I was the spoiled baby of the family'. Being the 'pampered baby' and completely spoiled meant I never experienced the same level of 'discipline' that my older brothers and sister experienced. I am certain if you were to ask any of them if that statement was true they would completely agree. Amazingly, even though I was spoiled and pampered during those years I always deeply respected my parents and was for the most part always a mild-mannered young boy, especially in public. Consequently, I was often allowed to be away from school to attend different functions with my parents, a lot of which were political functions they were invited to attend. Once again, at most of these events I would be the only child in attendance which usually led to me once again becoming the center of attention. All this continual 'attention' led to my being rewarded time and again with an abundance of 'gifts'. I have to admit this continual supply of material things as a young boy greatly helped to form my thoughts as to what my life would look like when I became an adult.

Fast forward a few years to when I first became a teenager. I was now fully permeated with a sense of 'entitlement' because of my earlier years of being so pampered and spoiled. I decided to join a local church youth group where many of my friends were already attending. This particular youth group was led by a young lady who was attending a nearby college. Leading the youth group was part of a 'work study' program the college offered that gave her extra credit in school for leading the 'group'. It's easy to see now that this young lady's primary purpose for leading the youth group was to earn extra credit in school, not to teach us about life, much less Christ.

Because I was so naïve, I never realized what was happening until it happened. At the age of fourteen I was swept up in a tornado of lust and youthful passion as this young lady sought me out and seduced me throughout the summer. At the beginning of the next school year our family moved to southern Arkansas, but at this point any and all discipline I might have had previously in my life was gone and I was basically out of control. By the time I turned fifteen I had begun experimenting with drugs and was already drinking alcohol. This continued into my life as an adult.

Fast forward again to my early days as a man living in south Texas. In several ways I exhibited many of the qualities of my father who was a WWII Veteran who raised me the best way he knew how. He never had much to do with church or religion which meant we never spoke of those things at all growing up. As a matter of fact, I can only remember a few times my father ever attended a church, and that was when I was still very young. Even so, he instilled within me a deep appreciation and respect for my elders which carried over into my life as an adult. Even though I struggled with drugs and alcohol, I attended church after church searching for something, that same 'thing' I was searching for as a young teenager when I was seduced by the teacher of the youth group. Eventually I just became too busy and caught up in life to realize it was in fact God Who was pursuing me and had an awesome and wonderful plan for my life. Looking back over the years I can now easily see how many times I missed seeing or understanding the 'signs' God had put right in front of me to lead me to Him. It's amazing looking back just how many times I can now see the Lord protected me and my family even though at the time we weren't serving Him at all. Now that is Amazing Grace!

I have often thought how much different my life might have been if I had somehow responded to the calling of the Lord when I was younger. I am just very, very grateful He never left me or gave up on me, but kept giving me multiple opportunities to say, 'Yes' to Jesus and finally start learning from the Holy Spirit how to live a disciplined, God-honoring life. I have to be honest and acknowledge I am at times a slow learner when it comes to living a disciplined life for the Lord. I am still daily learning how to be diligent and disciplined in seeking the Lord in His Word, speaking to Him continuously, and to 'see' Him in the details of how He is working in and through my life. It's a process, but it's the best days of my life!

Reading the Word every day is one of the best ways I have found to practice discipline and get stronger in my walk with the Lord. I just wish I were consistently more relentless in my personal pursuit of the Lord, His presence, His anointing, His Truth, His power and His will in my life. Possibly you are one who feels the same way as I often do. If so, we can thank the Lord He is patient with us and will never stop giving us every opportunity to come to Him. If you are struggling with 'discipline' in your life, then I challenge you to take a few moments, open the Word of God and read for a while. Ask the Holy Spirit to speak to your heart through the words you read. One thing I now love about His Word is that it is so direct and personal to me. Whenever I read His Word, He seems to always open my ears to hear the perfect words I need to hear for whatever I am facing that day. Thank You, Lord!

My dear heavenly Father, thank You for sending Your only Son, Jesus, to be my Savior. Thank You for covering and protecting me all those years I blindly walked apart from Your Word and Your will in my life. Thank You for Your undeniable love for me. Help me to continue to grow in being a disciple of Your Son, Jesus Christ. Help me to continue to live a lifestyle of holy disciplines reading Your Word, proclaiming Your truth, telling others about Your Son, my Savior and being led by the blessed Holy Spirit. Keep me from straying from Your presence, Your guidance, Your will and Your Word. Help me to always be a man who is recognized as one who READS THE WORD, SPEAKS THE WORD AND LIVES THE WORD! In Jesus' mighty Name I ask this.

Chapter Eight
ENDURANCE,
PERSERVERANCE and
DILIGENCE

Job 17:9 The righteous keep moving forward, and those with clean hands become stronger and stronger.

Psalm 37:24 Though they stumble, they will never fall, for the LORD holds them by the hand.

Psalm 73:24 You guide me with your counsel, leading me to a glorious destiny.

For some time now we've been discussing at our church the importance of obtaining and maintaining diligence, perseverance and endurance in each of our lives. Let's take a closer look at how Webster's dictionary defines each of these crucially important words:

- ENDURANCE - The ability to deal with pain and suffering that continues for a long time; the quality of continuing for a long time; the ability to do something difficult for a long time; the quality of continuing for a long time.

- PERSEVERANCE - Continued effort to do or achieve something despite difficulties, failures, or opposition; the action or condition or an instance of persevering;

- DILIGENCE - Persevering application; the attention and care legally expected or required of a person.

Wow! Looking at those definitions causes me to ask, 'Can you really have one without the other in your walk with Christ'? This reminds me of when I first began working in the management field many years ago. In those early days of management, I was strongly encouraged to make time to read a book called *The Five-Minute Manager.* Those who were in management over me assured me that the information in that book had the potential to direct me down a successful path to becoming a strong manger with an amazing future. If that's true in the corporate world, then it's even more TRUE if I were to make time to read and apply the principles in God's Word. After all, the Bible is the inspired, infallible Living Word of God, so it stands to reason if I make the time to read and study its inspired pages it will put me on the right path to becoming the strongest and most effective Christian I can be, right? Right!

Today I am convinced that without endurance, perseverance and diligence actively functioning in our lives it is impossible to ever become everything God has designed and created us to be for His glory. These are critical building blocks of the Holy Spirit to help us become those children that bring pleasure to our Heavenly Father and glory to our risen Lord. Yet, how many times (even in my own life) do I see us trying to circumvent these necessary qualities looking instead for some easier, quicker way to pleasing the Lord. It's amazing how those easier, quicker ways never work. I feel certain each of you can relate to what I am saying. How often have you become so comfortable in your routine with the Lord that you allowed your daily activities to take priority over your commitment and time with the Lord? That's the easier, quicker way to 'look' like a Christian, but not walk, talk and live like Christ. Ouch! What's surprising is this can all happen in seemingly the blink of an eye. The second you neglect endurance, perseverance and diligence in your walk of faith, compromise sneaks in and apathy takes over. One week you are walking in righteousness pleasing to the Lord, the next you are making excuses not to go to church, read your Bible or even spend time talking to the Lord.

We all have emotionally up and down days. Some of those 'days' we 'feel' like enduring, persevering and being diligent. However, if we were all honest, I think we would agree that most of our 'days' we really don't 'feel' like doing those things, but know in our hearts we 'need' to keep doing those things. Hebrews 4:15 tells us that even Jesus was tempted IN ALL THINGS LIKE AS WE ARE. Wow! That means even Jesus had days His flesh didn't 'feel' like enduring, persevering or being diligent, but He still pressed onward and upward overcoming every compromising 'feeling'. Hallelujah! That also means He knows exactly what we 'feel' like on those same difficult days, and if we simply trust Him, He also knows exactly how to OVERCOME and CONQUER every 'compromising 'feeling' we are facing in this moment!

So, endurance, perseverance and diligence MUST be willingly applied to our daily walk of faith if we are to become those obedient children of God who OVERCOME and CONQUER our 'feelings' which will NEVER lead us down a sustainable path of righteousness. The bottom line is: IT'S A CHOICE! We each have to be DETERMINED to CHOOSE that no matter what may be going on in our lives we are going to APPLY ourselves to SEEKING FIRST THE KINGDOM OF GOD AND

HIS RIGHTEOUSNESS (Matthew 6:33). For those who CHOOSE this path PERSEVERANCE will help keep you on the straight and narrow, DILIGENCE will help to supply much needed STRENGTH which will result in the God-given ability to ENDURE whatever may come.

Personally, whenever I am DAILY DILIGENT in those things, I unquestionably know God expects of me, then I find myself consistently 'growing' in the grace and knowledge of our Lord Jesus (2 Peter 3:18). Furthermore, whenever I choose to push through my fickle feelings and PERSEVERE, I find it much easier to discern and HEAR God's voice above all the other voices warring for my attention. Oh, how glorious is the mercy of God which offers forgiveness to those who repent for all those times our weaknesses win the moment and lead us into compromise and sin. Oh, how glorious is His promise to 'never leave us or forsake us'. Praise the Lord! With God on my side, I really don't care who or what comes against me.

Heavenly Father, I acknowledge that I am still extremely weak and in desperate need of endurance, diligence and perseverance in so many areas of my life. Honestly, I feel as though I have so little endurance I am void of any true spiritual prowess and of no threat or danger to enemy of our souls. My lack of perseverance causes it to appear as though I have no interest whatsoever for Your Word or presence. What little diligence I display looks more like a roller coaster ride than an arrow piercing the bullseye of the target. Oh God, please forgive me again and help me to consistently seek and find You in all I do or say. My life is nothing more than a barren fruit tree without Your presence, Your voice, Your strength, Your forgiveness, Your patience, Your love and Your guidance. Thank You for giving me a heart that truly longs to run this race and win this fight for Your glory. Thank You for Your continual patience with me. Thank You for always being there every time I find myself weak and in need of Your strength. I love You, Lord with all my heart. Help me to serve You with an enduring, persevering and diligent life of obedience and love. In Jesus name I pray.

Chapter Nine
Attacks

1 Peter 5:8 Stay alert! Watch out for your great enemy, the devil. He prowls around like a roaring lion, looking for someone to devour.

Throughout my life I have often been viewed as somewhat of a simple, straightforward man due to the way I tend to look at things. I've always been a 'matter of fact' guy who views things based on what is right in front of me rather than on what 'might be'. Consequently, it was not uncommon for others to label me a 'country boy', which is something I've chosen to view as a term of endearment. As a Christian I am no different. Things just aren't that complex the way I see them. Either you live your life 'for' the Lord or 'against' Him, it's really not rocket science. That's why I simply, but also openly and unashamedly let others know I am honored, proud and humbled to be a Christian. Of course, I don't always say things perfectly and I can with certainty tell you I am definitely NOT politically correct. Even so, it's never my goal or intention to purposefully offend anyone (other than the devil), but to instead be honest and upfront with them always speaking what I know to be the truth. Consequently, should anything I say in these writings offend you in any way, please know that was never my intention even though it's completely possible I will say something inappropriate for today's 'love everyone just the way they are' culture. My only purpose for writing these experiences is to somehow bless and encourage you in your walk with the Lord.

I may not be famous on any front, but my name is written in the Lamb's Book of Life and my heavenly Father calls me by my first name. That means I am important to the Lord, and in my view that makes my life important enough to share with others. So, the experiences I am sharing in these pages are things I truly believe have been given to me from the Lord to share with each of you.

Because I am 'important' to the Lord, that also makes me in a real sense a target for the enemies of God. It shouldn't come as a surprise to any of you, then, that my family and I have experienced many, many ATTACKS from God's enemies through the years. Sadly, it took a long time for us to finally begin realizing that many of the ATTACKS coming against us were from hell rather than from any person we were having issues with either in the family or elsewhere. It took us a long time to understand whenever any individual 'attacks' us verbally, personally, financially or otherwise it's really not them doing the attacking, but the enemy (satan) manipulating them to come against us.

Ephesians 6:12 For we are not fighting against flesh-and-blood enemies, but against evil rulers and authorities of the unseen world, against mighty powers in this dark world, and against evil spirits in the heavenly places.

Honestly, it's difficult to admit, but it wasn't until Tuesday morning, May 14, 2013, that I finally understood where all the 'crap' (if I may use that term) was coming from. Thankfully, after two years of being in a 'real' relationship with the Lord, the Light finally came on and I could clearly see the majority of the attacks were centered around our children. For years I watched as our oldest child and daughter endured what seemed like countless brutal attacks on her character at school. She also unknowingly had relationships with guys that would suddenly become abusive. To be totally honest, by today's standards there was even a season in her life I would have been labelled an abusive father. Looking back, I can only say that during that season I was doing the best I knew how to do as a parent who loves their child and wants the best for her. By God's grace those days are over and our relationship today is as good as it has ever been. I am (and always have been) very proud of her as she has not only survived the attacks, but has fought and won with the Lord in her life. Thank You, Jesus! Today we are seeing wonderful changes in many areas of her life, as well as seeing a sparkle in her eye that is brighter than ever before.

Thankfully our youngest son had a fairly uneventful childhood in regard to facing a lot of attacks or abuse. He was one of those kids that pretty much stayed to himself and out of any serious trouble. That quickly changed once he became an adult, got married and started having children of his own. It seemed like satan was sticking his nose in all our son's affairs which resulted in divorce, long-term financial struggles, multiple speeding tickets, and other issues that continue to haunt him today. Even so, he still graduated with honors at UTI (Universal Technical Institute) in Houston, Texas. Today he is remarried and now has five children.

Of course, my relationship with my precious wife, Karen, is a miracle as well as mystery. Why she chose to stay through all the troubled years of our marriage I will never fully understand. All I can say is I am so grateful to her and the Lord she stuck it out with me. We were both raised to fight for the people and things we believe in and love most, and our marriage was worth the fight. That's right! Marriage is a fight, and that's exactly what we've done through the years fighting at times with each other, but now fighting for each other. Today we have a completely new and exciting outlook for our marriage as we are together fighting the good fight of faith. I don't believe you ever quit learning and evolving in a marriage. In our earlier years of marriage, we had no idea we were at times fighting the demons in hell who were trying to destroy our marriage, our family and ultimately our lives. We just thought we were living the life we were dealt. One huge issue we had in our early years was my trouble with alcohol. In Texas all the good ole boys are expected to have a beer in their hand, and that was me. I was what is referred to as a functioning alcoholic. I held down a steady (and good) job, took the kids to all their events and planned our family vacations. Yet, all the while I was almost always inebriated. Almost everywhere I went I was under the influence of alcohol. I can tell you this with certainty since I grew up in a family environment wherein my father lived the same way. Eventually my father became an alcohol and drug abuse counselor because of his own personal demons he lived with for so long.

My wife fought depression for years. We know that we understand satan's strategy in all this we no longer are under the power and influence of alcohol or depression. Instead, we are now living our lives as overcomers placing our faith, trust and future in God's hands knowing in Christ 'no weapon formed against us will prosper'.

I want to share one more struggle from the past with you in hopes it will help any of you who may be facing the same fight today. It was around 2005 and there's no other way to say it, wickedness and evil had a strong grip on me and my family. To make matters worse (in my mind) my employer issued me a mandatory work phone with the last four digits being 6669. Every time I saw that number all I could think about was satan. What a mess I was! Then, to make matters worse, in 2008 our home burned down. Over the next several months we moved from hotel to hotel where it seemed 'evil' followed us everywhere we went. We've always been dog people, so the first hotel we went to didn't allow pets. Once we finally found a hotel, we could all stay in, well, it was infested with bed bugs. They were so bad I ended up with severe staph infections on my back. The next hotel seemed great until we had to move out due to the dogs barking whenever we would be gone working. Finally, we were able to find an apartment in Humble, Texas where as long as we walked out dogs on a leash everything was good. Then one day one of our dogs ran out the door before we could catch him and, of course the management saw him running around which soon led to us having to move across the street to yet another apartment complex that was much more pet friendly at the time. We remained in that complex six years, but were progressively being harassed about our dogs by the consistently ever-changing management. With each new manager came a completely new set of rules that almost always put us behind the eight ball in respect to our family pets. The more this occurred the more agitated I became until Tuesday, May 14, 2013. It was around 5:30 a.m. and I was getting ready for work while Karen was making breakfast (something she did everyday) for me. As I was eating breakfast and watching the news, she informed me about a bill for a parking ticket from 2005 that had come in the mail. With all the fines and delinquent payment charges the bill was now $454.00 for a simple parking ticket. We briefly discussed the bill, then I left for work. While driving that morning alone in my truck everything we had been going through came crashing in sending me into both depression and anger. All I could think about in those moments was I WAS DONE with everything! As I entered the freeway quickly getting up to speed, I immediately passed an 18-wheeler. Suddenly I heard a voice telling me to change lanes and place myself directly in front of the large truck I had just passed, then slam on my brakes. Then all my troubles would be over in an instant. THEN SOMETHING HAPPENED THAT CHANGED MY LIFE FOREVER! In that moment I clearly heard another, more powerful Voice say, 'Not today, satan. It's not his time and you can't have him'. In that single instant I KNEW GOD WAS IN MY TRUCK WITH ME! Then all the depression instantly left and a huge smile erupted on my face. All the years of trouble, bad decisions and willful sin still hadn't been enough to keep the Lord away from being IN MY TRUCK. I almost made a stupid, life-changing mistake that morning, but God intervened and changed my life forever! Thank You, Jesus!

Today my wife and I have learned to take a stand and proclaim, 'satan, you can't have our family anymore. Our family is covered by the blood of Jesus Christ our Lord and Savior. If you want us, then you have to go through Him and His blood to get to us, and that just ain't going to ever happen.'

Attacks are real, and the enemy who initiates far more of these attacks than you might ever believe is real, too. If you are at the end of your rope and ready to do something stupid, then call out to Jesus right now. He is in the truck with you and ready to fight on your behalf for your life, your family, your health, your finances and your salvation. Don't let pride keep you from reaching out to Him right now. You can't do this alone! No one can! Don't wait another moment. Surrender to Jesus and let Him show you how to drive out the enemy and keep him from destroying everything that is precious to you. Jesus has conquered once for all the power of satan and stands ready to set you and your family free. Who wouldn't want Him to help them in their darkest hour see all the darkness, despair and depression be gone and a smile come on their face?

Father in heaven, I thank you for everything You do, everything You've ever done, and all You are yet to do for in the days to come. Oh, how I pray You would continue to give us a courageous heart to fight the good fight of faith and never again be overwhelmed or conquered by the evil, wicked schemes of the enemy. Oh, how I pray our lives will bring You glory, honor and praise in the days to come. Your love is such a vast and impenetrable canopy that can never be pierced, diminished or destroyed. May we forever remain under the canopy of Your protection and love until the Day we see You face to face. In Jesus' name I pray.

Chapter Ten
Spirits

Ephesians 6:14 Stand your ground, putting on the belt of truth and the body armor of God's righteousness.

Although I'm no expert on 'spirits', I feel the need to share some of my personal perspectives on angels and spirits that accompany our daily walk with the Lord. I was greatly encouraged writing about this topic and pray each of you find the same encouragement the Lord has given me through this 'country boy's' thoughts. Before I start this topic, I have to say that in this moment I am so overwhelmed with the goodness of our mighty God I feel I just have to shout out loud, GOD IS GOOD! JESUS IS ALIVE! THANK YOU, LORD! HALLELUJAH!

To begin this chapter, we need to travel back several years to the months before I finally committed my life to Jesus Christ as my Lord and Savior. My wife, Karen, and I were like millions of other Americans who knew of Jesus and even occasionally went to church, but Jesus was not front and center in our lives or our thoughts. At the time we were pursuing purchasing our 'forever' home. Consequently, our time and lives were consumed with exploring different areas looking for the perfect home for us, one that lined up with the things we were both interested in having in our 'forever' home. If you've ever gone through this process you know how exhausting, but also exhilarating it can be as you painstakingly consider all the different school districts, proximity to our favorite stores, closeness to necessary medical facilities, size of lots, age and price of each property, etc. It's shocking to look back and realize how at the time we never considered closeness to a church family (much less closeness to the Lord) as part of the criteria for buying our 'forever' home. That is really sad, but it's also part of the 'spirit' that permeates millions of homes still today, homes wherein Jesus can be a topic of discussion, but where He is quickly forgotten when discussing or focusing on the things we want in life.

As Karen and I continued our search for our 'forever' home we talked about both liking the idea of living in a smaller community even though we both worked in the bustling metropolis of Houston, the fourth largest city in our nation. Our first serious consideration began in Atascocita, a small suburb about 20 miles north of Houston. 20 miles is considered a short drive to work in this area, so we knew we would be lucky to find a home we both loved and could afford that close to the big city. After driving around the area and looking at several different homes, we finally found one we liked enough to inquire further about. We immediately called the realtor who had the home listed and were able to set up a viewing later that afternoon. We decided to use the couple of hours prior to meeting the realtor to check out the surrounding areas closest to the neighborhood where we were possibly going to be living. We already loved the immediate neighborhood which was quiet and at first glance seemingly a good place to raise our family. We were so excited we might have found our 'forever' home we arrived early for our appointment with the realtor. We parked in the driveway, then decided to go ahead and walk around the outside of the house while we waited for the realtor to arrive. Soon we were in the backyard and became even more excited as we imagined our children growing up in the large, expansive backyard that also offered ample safety and security. At that moment the realtor arrived and we couldn't wait to see the inside of the home. Of course, we had to stand outside and patiently listen as the realtor gave her sales pitch about the home, the neighborhood and the surrounding area before she opened the lock and allowed us to enter the home. As she unlocked and then opened the door, being raised to be a gentleman, I held the door as the two women entered the empty residence first. Once we were all inside, closing the door behind me we quickly made our way into the living room. Suddenly and quite unexpectedly I was stopped dead in my tracks as an overwhelming feeling swarmed over my entire being. The hair on my neck, back and arms instantly stood straight up as an icy, cold chill ran down my spine. At the time I had no idea what was happening, but all I knew was I had to get out of that place as quickly as possible. I instantly dug my heels into the carpet, made a fast turn around and exited the residence within seconds. I walked straight to my truck and stood there nervously twiddling my thumbs. Moments later Karen and the realtor called for me to come and look at the beautiful bedroom. I yelled back, 'I'm outside and never going back into that home'. That response caused the realtor to come outside and ask me, 'What is wrong?' I replied, 'Something terrible happened in that home or else something very evil is in there and I don't want any part of the home'. The agent looked at me in bewilderment, as though I were crazy, but in that moment, I honestly didn't care what she thought about me. I simply wanted to get Karen in the truck and get out of there as soon as possible. Knowing something was really bothering me, Karen got in the truck, we quickly thanked the agent for her time, then left.

That happened at a time in my life when I had no understanding at all of evil spirits and how they can actually dwell in a physical place and relentlessly torment people who are unaware of their presence or existence. That was one of my first experiences with evil 'spirits' and I am thankful that today I know who and what they are, where they came from, why they are here, and that Jesus has overcome every one of them. Thank You, Jesus!

Luke 10:19 Look, I have given you authority over all the power of the enemy, and you can walk among snakes and scorpions and crush them. Nothing will injure you.

Thank you, Father God, for Your faithfulness to keep and protect us even when we have no understanding of what is happening in the moment. Thank You for Your guidance, and for giving me the sensitivity to discern and even feel the presence of evil 'spirits' around me and my family. I pray that everyone gets to a place in their walk with You that they are able to discern and feel the presence of evil 'spirits' around them and their families, but also know there is nothing to fear for You have given Your children Your authority to overcome by the blood of the Lamb, Jesus Christ. Hallelujah and Amen! In Jesus name I pray.

Chapter Eleven
Relationship

Romans 3:23 For everyone has sinned. We all fall short of God's glorious standard.

It's important to me that you understand I'm not targeting any specific individual in the following comments, but in truth talking about every one of us. If I were to 'target' any single individual it would be ME. I need and long for a closer, more vibrant walk with the Lord, and am just thinking this topic may be just as important to some of you as it is to me.

Do any of you ever feel like your relationship with the Lord is much like riding a roller coaster day after day after day? Mine certainly feels like that most days as my walk with the Lord is up and down, then up and down again! Considering this reminds me of the time when as a young boy I became a member of a small local church in Iowa. It wasn't long before I was singing in the choir and getting involved in many of the church activities each week.

Then all that radically changed when we moved to Arkansas. After getting settled in our new town I began visiting several small churches in the area. Honestly, my main reason for going to church was to find the 'good' girls in town. It didn't take long before I was going to church less and less choosing to do a number of other non-church activities that made going to church inconvenient. That kind of up and down relationship with 'going to church' lingered all the way through my high school years. Shortly after graduating from High School I moved to Texas, or as we like to say, 'God's Country'.

Well, you guessed it. After moving to God's Country my up and down relationship with 'church' remained exactly that, Up and Down. I attended many churches through the years until we finally found a small church that actually is based on 'relationship' with each other and with the Lord. In this church, my church, we all lovingly hold each other accountable for our relationship with the Lord. What a crazy idea, huh? To actually make 'going to church' about 'RELATIONSHIP' rather than just programs! Before becoming part of the family at The FORT Discipleship Center I guess you would have to say I conveniently kept my dance card always full, at least in my eyes. That kind of thinking allowed me to keep running from the Lord and His will and purpose for my life. After years of running and hiding from the Lord's call the Holy Spirit unexpectedly and mercifully took hold of my heart and mind in a little church smack dab in the middle of God's Country. My life, marriage and family have never been the same since that glorious day.

So, let me ask: What do you believe it takes to obtain and maintain a meaningful RELATIONSHIP?

Webster's Dictionary:
- the way in which two or more people, groups, countries, etc. talk to, behave toward, and deal with one another;
- the way in which two or more people or things are connected;
- a romantic or sexual friendship between two people

(note: That Websters dictionary didn't differentiate that a relationship should be between a man and woman.)

The TRUTH is, having the opportunity to be in 'relationship' with anyone originated with the Lord. He is the Creator and Master Designer of 'relationship'. So, I have to ask, what kind of relationship do you currently have with the Lord, the Author of relationships? Is your relationship with Him one-sided and all about you, your wants, your desires, your way, your hopes, your dreams or even your complaints? Do you come and go from His presence when it seems good to you, or do you seek Him continually because He longs to be in relationship with you? Would you say your relationship with Him is pleasing to Him? I would love to think everyone I know is pleasing to the Lord, but we all know that simply isn't the case. *Romans 3:23* tells us, 'For everyone has sinned; we all fall short of God's glorious standard' For those of you who are married, simply think of those times you've fallen short of the expectations of your husband or wife. I can't begin to tell you how many times I've fallen short in my relationship with my wife woefully missing the mark set by the Lord for every husband. The fact is we ALL FALL SHORT at some point in every relationship, but especially in our relationship with the Lord. My wife deserves a husband who is dedicated and committed to being the best example of a Godly husband he can be, and I am determined by God's grace to be that man. That's the HARD, but right choice. Falling short and simply accepting that kind of relationship is the EASY way and far too many take that 'easy' road today which always ends up in destruction.

Possibly you are 'relating' to the Lord the way I did for many years. Maybe the Lord doesn't 'fit' into your current plans, schedule or lifestyle, so you conveniently have chosen to simply not make much of an effort to spend time with Him. Wow! I can't believe I once thought that way about the Lord Who not only created me, but longs to be in a personal relationship with me, but on His terms, not mine. He is always ready to forgive, forget and lovingly pour out His blessings if I am willing to simply come to Him in a real, honest and personal way. His love covers a multitude of sins (falling short time and time again) and He forgives all those times we fall short casting them as far as the East is from the West when we ask Him for mercy and forgiveness. He loves you more than you could ever comprehend or imagine, and His love is unconditional. That simply means there is nothing you could do that would cause Him to not still love you. Yet, His unconditional Love is never a condoning Love when it comes to sin (falling short). He loves us too much to allow us to live controlled by sin, fear, hatred, greed or lust. Being in relationship with Him means He becomes the Source of stability and strength for the relationship which insures it will last forever. If you do not have a personal relationship with Him, then call out to Him in this moment. He will hear your heart, heal your heart, change your heart and give you His heart from now unto eternity.

Heavenly Father, thank You for Your patience, mercy, forgiveness and love. I pray my relationship with You continues to grow and strengthen through Your Word, Your presence and Your blessed Holy Spirit. May You ever Light my path and lead me on the straight and narrow Way, Your Way. Should I start to ever become lazy again in my relationship with You, do whatever is necessary to get my attention and bring me back into a vibrant relationship with You. I pray this in Jesus' name.

Chapter Twelve
SETBACKS

Romans 5:3 We can rejoice, too, when we run into problems and trials, for we know that they help us develop endurance.

Webster's dictionary defines 'setback' as: a problem that makes progress more difficult or success less likely.

Taking that definition at face value, does it bring to mind any obvious 'setbacks' in your life right now? I know it does for me. Now I have to ask, 'Where do you think the majority of these setbacks originate?' Are they just bad decisions, bad luck or could they even be the result of something wicked and sinister going on in your life? Remember, we all commonly experience setbacks in life. Does each setback represent being overwhelmed and defeated in that moment? I can't say the answer is that simple, but I am confident how we handle the setbacks is what ultimately defines us as either overcomers or victims.

I think we can all agree setbacks come in all sizes with some being far more impactful in our lives than others. Learning to correctly handle the smaller, minor setbacks will greatly determine how you handle the life-altering, major setbacks. So, I have to another question: How would you say you are doing in handling the minor setbacks in your life? Possibly you are one who has experienced a major setback recently in your life. How are you fairing through it all? Has it completely dominated your life or are you learning how to 'endure' through it all for the glory of our Father in heaven? Maybe you are one of the millions who recently lost your job due to the COVID 19 pandemic. How are you handling being jobless possibly for the first time in many years? Has the stress of it all caused you to start drinking in an effort to relieve the worry and fear of the unknown? Could it be you are one who becomes so overwhelmed with the stress of a major setback you simply crawl up in your bed and stay in your room for days. Each of those avenues presents some momentary solace, but they never solve the problem or get rid of the setback. Do drink yourself into a stupor as I once did? Once the alcohol wears off or you can't sleep any more, the setback is still lingering and still haunting your thoughts.

I have no idea if it's the same with you, but in my life, setbacks seem to come in bunches and always seem to last for months. As I look back on my earlier days whenever the setbacks would start coming and coming, my outlet was to find a quiet place and start attacking the pain and confusion with alcohol. One beer would quickly lead into another, and another, and another until my senses were so pickled nothing bothered me for a while. Everything was fine until I sobered up. Then it seemed as though the thoughts came even quicker and more severe, so I went right back out and got drunk again to soften the pain. Thankfully, I no longer look to alcohol as a solution for anything, but that still doesn't mean that every time I experience a setback, I automatically handle it the right way. It really does take time, God's word, God's presence and mountains of His grace to work your way through some setbacks. The great news is there has never been any setback that was too big for God to handle or get me through. Learning to lean on the Lord for His help allowing Him to carry the heavy burdens that often come from setbacks has been life-changing.

If you are facing overwhelming circumstances that have resulted in a major setback in your life, then look to Jesus to guide you through the 'valley of the shadow of death' to the still waters of His peace and safety. He is right there with you ready to intervene and drive out the devil who has been harassing you far too long.

My dear heavenly Father, please give me the strength and grace to handle every problem and setback in my life. Give me wisdom to handle them in such a way that is pleasing to You. Help me to run with endurance the race of this life to win and never be disqualified. Help me see and understand that no setback ever takes You by surprise, but instead You have supplied everything I need to overcome the fear, worry and doubt and finish the race victoriously for Your glory and praise. In Jesus' Name I pray.

Chapter Thirteen

MYSTERIOUS

Psalm 102:28 The children of Your people will live in security. Their children's children will thrive in Your presence.

It's interesting to see how some things have so dramatically changed from the time I was a young boy. For instance, when I was still very young it was not unusual at all for my parents, who deeply loved me, to leave me alone in the house while they ran errands or had to work. If that same thing were to occur today the child would be taken from the home and the parents prosecuted for negligence. I'm not advocating leaving young children at home alone, but those days 'back then' were much different than today. When I was a young boy there was a completely different family environment which established a confidence and trust factor most families don't possess today. I grew up in a wonderful, wholesome family environment full of trust, peace, love and confidence. Discipline in the home was a big part of that foundation. Kids were expected to 'mind their parents'. Whenever you didn't 'mind your parents' there was the expectation of certain and swift punishment for their willing rebellion. I can still hear the words being said, 'Do as I say, not as I do'.

I've mentioned in earlier chapters that my family was not a 'religious' family and seldom ever went to church. However, back in those days the fabric of our society was greatly affected by a common 'belief' in God, His Word, His love and His judgment. Consequently, even for families such as mine there were still times when 'faith' significantly factored into the choices and actions made within the family unit. As I now reflect back on those days I am overwhelmed by the mercy, love and goodness of our great God. It is absolutely undeniable God was continuously at work even in my family influencing my parents and establishing in their hearts a solid 'faith' and 'trust' in the Him to keep and protect me whenever they would be gone for hours leaving me home alone. I am confident had they not believed that everything would be just fine, they would have never left me alone.

I'm particularly drawn to the summer of 1967. My parents, grandmother and I went on a wonderful vacation to Mexico. After returning home I went to stay with my sister who lived in the country. At the time I was six years of age (turning seven in August). My parents were hard workers working every day of the week which made it very difficult for either of them to get away to do extra activities with me during the summer. Therefore, they thought it would be a great idea for me to be with my sister and her husband in the country for the summer. The general consensus was I would have a lot more freedom to do a lot more 'fun' things staying in the country, even though my sister and her husband both worked day jobs, too. At that early age I was still very obedient and listened to the wishes of my parents. However, I was also a very inquisitive young boy who was always on the lookout for something to keep my mind and body engaged and active.

My sister and her husband owned and operated a service station in Louisburg,

Kansas which was about 40 miles outside of Kansas City. That was back in the days before self-service became the rage, which meant they pumped the gas, checked the oil, checked the tire pressure, washed the windows and took care of the payment for every customer. Even so, there were some days my sister would stay home with me, but oftentimes she would have to go in with her husband when the workload was especially heavy. On those 'heavy work' days when both my sister and her husband were gone, I had six four-legged companions who chaperoned me throughout my day. First there was Chocolate, a smallish wiry dog with a short white and chocolate colored hair. Then there was Gigi and Pierre, two poodles who were both really feisty and playful. Then there was Penny and Lucky. Lucky probably had some Spitz in his blood which gave him a very protective personality. Lastly, there was Brutus. You would think with a name like Brutus he would be a dominant and fearsome animal who was the alpha of the entire group. Instead, he was a gentle, sweet dog who was my friend and was always happy to be with me.

Consequently, with six dogs and a house full of cats (living in the country everyone had cats to keep down the mice population) my sister and my parents weren't concerned at all for my safety whenever I had to stay at the house alone. Another thing that made it easier was the fact I was always a kid who was an 'old soul' acting much older than my age. Maybe that had something to do with having older parents and an older sister. Anyway, even on those days my sister would have to go to work, she would only be gone for a short while to get the workload organized, then head back home to take care of me. On one particular day, however, she got caught at work a little longer than she had planned and was gone for several hours. For some reason that was the day I decided I wanted to go fishing in the pond on the property. It was a fairly large farm pond and was easily seen from the house. The water was always clear and, on this day, it sparkled like it had diamonds floating on it. Even though I was only six years of age, after only a few minutes I was able to find the fishing poles and tackle box. Without hesitating I grabbed a pole and the tackle box and headed for the pond that was mysteriously calling my name. I imagine the whole thing looked much like an episode of Andy Griffith as I skipped down the path to the pond. As expected, I wasn't alone as I headed out for the adventure of the day. Pierre, the smallest of all the protectors, decided to join me as I headed out to conquer whatever Leviathan might be lurking in the pond. The pond was about 200 yards from the house down a dirt path with tall grass on either side of the path. Pierre and I had nothing but fishing on our minds as we scampered down the path completely unsuspecting of anything happening. As we excitedly approached the edge of the pond Pierre suddenly jumped in front of me and became extremely agitated and aggressive growling and barking at some unseen intruder. I had no idea what was happening and had never heard such sounds as were coming out of little Pierre that moment. Even so, after a couple of minutes I decided to try and go around Pierre to get to the water, but Pierre would have none of it and stayed between me and whatever was in front of him. Then I heard the unmistakable rattling sound of an angry rattlesnake just out of sight, but directly ahead where I would have walked. I still get chills thinking about the sound of that rattlesnake. In an instant I turned and rapidly started making my way back to the safety of the house all the while calling Pierre to follow me. Thankfully, once he saw I was retreating to safety he happily followed me back to the house.

It's amazing and wondrous to look back on that day and realize how the Lord had set His sentinels around me for my protection and safety. That day the Lord used Pierre to save a little boy's life. It would be impossible to calculate how many times the Lord has moved us out of harm's way when unseen enemies were waiting to ambush our lives and steal, kill or destroy everything precious to us. What a mighty, faithful and awesome God we have!

Thank You, Lord for creating me with a heavenly PLAN for my life. Thank you for the safety and protection You've continually provided me throughout my entire lifetime. Thank You for being a covenant-keeping Savior Who never takes a day off from loving, keeping, protecting and preserving Your children. I pray that the eyes of all my brothers and sisters in Christ would be opened to see Your loving protection and provision and how You have set heavenly sentinels around us to help guard, lead and protect us as we travel through these momentary, but at times dangerous days. I pray my walk with You brings the praise and glory You so deserve for all You do to guide, protect, lead, teach and provide for me and my family. Oh, how I long to share with others all You continue to share with me. I love You, Lord. In Jesus' name I pray.

Chapter Fourteen
Referral

Matthew 10:32 Everyone who acknowledges Me publicly here on earth, I will also acknowledge before My Father in heaven.

It is crucial for companies that supply any type of 'service' to the general public to maintain and build upon a 'good reputation' in their immediate community. Consequently, it is customary for companies to regularly request our help through filling out surveys answering a few questions centered around our recent visit to their business. They do this to amass data which gives them a better understanding of how they can improve their services to us, the consumers. A perfect example of this is the last time I went to our local hardware store. After making my purchase I noticed a request for a survey on the receipt. To 'thank' me for taking the few moments necessary to complete the survey, I was assured my name would be entered into a drawing for future discounts and rewards. So far, I haven't heard whether or not my name was drawn, but hopefully the information I supplied will help them stay in business during these trying times.

Another experience my wife and I recently had with a 'service' based company was my latest visit to our chiropractor. I regularly visit his office due to past 'work related' injuries. First, let me say how grateful we are to have found this chiropractor because we both really appreciate his outlook and wisdom concerning chiropractic medicine. Also, after our first visit we discovered he is a professing Christian who has a sincere desire is to help the physical body do exactly what the Lord created it to do, heal itself. How refreshing to find a business where you sincerely enjoy and appreciate the 'service' they offer and render. Because we truly 'like' the chiropractor and trust in what he says and does, we spontaneously promote this 'business' to others who need a chiropractor. This is exactly what 'service' oriented businesses rely upon, word of mouth testimonies that spread throughout the community setting in motion an automatic chain-reaction of public approval that is better than any ad campaign a company could pay for. It doesn't matter if it's a restaurant, doctor, veterinarian, grocery store or car wash, if your experience is a really good one, then you will automatically tell those you know. It's the proverbial 'grape vine' effect every company longs to see take place with their business.

Think about the last time you tried a new restaurant and had a 'great' experience. How long did it take you to tell your friends and family they should 'try' that same restaurant? Probably not long at all, and I'm fairly certain it wasn't long before you were back there for another visit. The truth is, without this kind of spontaneous neighborhood 'referral grapevine', these types of businesses would not remain in business very long. It reminds me of *Proverbs 18:21* **which states, *'The tongue can bring death or life; those who love to talk will reap the consequences.'*** There was a time not too long ago when this type of neighborhood 'referral grapevine' was in fact spontaneous and done simply out of gratitude for a 'business environment' that resulted in a great experience for the whole family. The 'great experience' was payment enough for the 'services' rendered. Things are much different today.

Businesses are now compelled to offer a variety of incentives, rewards, promised future benefits or discounts for your positive remarks about your experience with their 'business' due to the ever-increasing volume of customers making online purchases. Although I understand the concept behind offering 'incentives' for a positive referral, this has in part led to an entire generation of younger adults who live with a 'what's in it for me' mentality. I can't help but wonder what their (our) response would be if the Lord sent us a survey concerning everything, He has done for us. What kind of questions would He ask? Again, I'm only imagining, but it might look something like this:

Hello My child. Thank you for visiting with Me today in church.
- Were you satisfied and blessed by everything that took place in the service?
- What did you think of the Word that was preached today?
- Did you find it awkward being asked to lift your hands in praise to Me?

- Did you find it difficult to pray directly to Me rather than have someone else pray for you?
- Did you find it offensive to be asked to give financially in the offering?
- Did you think the preacher focused too much on holiness, righteousness and obedience to My words rather than on your personal happiness?
- When the Holy Spirit began moving among the people did you begin to feel nervous or uncomfortable?
- I noticed you were on your phone a lot and not really paying attention to the message. Was there something more important you needed to take care of or were you simply bored in the service?
- During the worship time I did see your mouth moving, but I couldn't hear any sounds coming out of your mouth. Were you too concerned about what others might think of your singing that you wouldn't sing out loud to Me?
- Can you think of anything else you would like Me to do for you in the service that I haven't already done through My Son, Jesus Christ?

I don't know why it seems to be easier for most of us to spontaneously talk to someone else about a great experience we had in a restaurant or some other kind of 'service-oriented' business, but we can't muster up enough courage to spontaneously speak of our awesome God Who sent His own Son to die for our sins. Wow! That makes no sense at all to me! Possibly it's because we are so connected with our feelings. We had a good experience in the restaurant which catered to our having a good 'feeling' about the place which led to our promoting the business based on our 'feelings' about the service 'we' received. That in a nutshell reveals the elephant in the room when it comes to 'church'. The Lord never created 'church' to be about us and our happiness, but He created CHURCH for Him and HIS GLORY! When we 'go to church' and judge our experience the same way we might a judge new restaurant, then we have missed the whole purpose, point and reason for going!

I know I have fallen far short of what God deserves and expects from my life. Instead of just accepting that, I want that to change, and CHANGE FOREVER. I sincerely desire to live for the honor and glory of my heavenly Father Who loves me so much He sent His only Son Jesus to die for me that I might live for Him. I am learning more and more that a real and meaningful relationship with the Lord touches and changes every part of your life, every part of your senses and every part of your dreams. You, too, can have that same relationship with the Lord, one that has the power to CHANGE YOU and make you NEW. If that's what you desire, then at this very moment just be honest with Him and talk to Him. Ask Him for forgiveness, but also for guidance and wisdom for the days ahead. If you approach Him with a sincere heart, then He will hear and answer you in ways that you will be able to clearly hear His voice speaking to your heart. Then you will taste and see the goodness and the salvation of God in your heart and others will see it manifest in your life. I am a witness of how He will take you out of your present darkness and transfer you into His marvelous Light where there is freedom and joy everlasting with Jesus.

My dear heavenly Father, I come before You in this moment humbly asking forgiveness for all my arrogance, pride and selfish choices that have too often resulted in my not bringing You honor and glory through my words or actions. From this moment forward may I be a man You find faithful, trustworthy and pleasing having placed everything in my life under Your care and control. Give me the courage and boldness to not be silent to others about Your love, mercy, kindness, forgiveness and patience You have faithfully shown toward me and my family. I want to be a neighborhood grapevine of You and Your love to all those I encounter throughout the day. May I do this spontaneously and expectantly believing my witness of Your goodness will draw others to Your Son, my Savior, Jesus Christ. I love You, Lord. I pray this in Your Son's mighty Name, Amen!

Chapter Fifteen
Unfinished!

Philippians 1:6 And I am certain that God, who began the good work within you, will continue His work until it is finally finished on the day when Christ Jesus returns.

When I first began my walk with Christ, I honestly thought from that point on my life in general would be much easier. I literally felt like I was walking on clouds those first few days, and therefore assumed everything in my life would somehow automatically follow that same pattern. Well, it didn't take long before I realized the strained relationships and circumstances that had been in my life for quite a while weren't automatically getting stronger or better just because I had surrendered my life to Christ. I had no idea what it really meant to walk with Christ day after day living my life by God's standards rather than everyone else's. It's amazing how easy it is to surround yourself with people who have no thought or desire to live for Christ, and how difficult it is to find a 'family' of brothers and sisters in Christ who long to live everyday of their lives for Him and His glory. No matter how hard I tried it seemed like the more I searched for people who had the same desire I had to live for Christ, the more I was bombarded with things that stirred up my old, unrighteous attitudes and emotions.

The fact is those who have never committed their lives to Christ have no clue what a sincere walk with Christ encompasses or looks like, nor do most of them really care. That's precisely why, no matter how difficult it may seem, you must make every effort to surround yourself with like-minded individuals who sincerely hunger to live their lives for Christ, too. Don't get me wrong, even finding what you believe is 'that family' of believers will not keep 'life' from still happening. We are all human and filled with all sorts of human weaknesses. You know exactly what I mean. How many times has 'life' happened while you were going about your daily business? I'm speaking of those times you are at the grocery store, doing yardwork, in a restaurant having a quiet meal or pumping gas and unexpectedly you are confronted by someone with a lousy attitude who are clearly not concerned at all with a Christ-like conduct. I actually can imagine that for most of you (as well as me) your first inclination is to be as pleasant as possible, but at the same time you are sensing in your heart something else is going on here. You might even ask yourself, 'Why did this person target me instead of so many others they could have confronted? Why were they being nice to others, but are being so belligerent to me?' If you're like me you hold it together pretty well for the first few moments, but as they persist your old fleshly nature starts getting heated up and the next thing you know your attitude goes south. By this time the atmosphere is one of anger and anxiety and the peace that was on you exits the premises. Once the whole ordeal is done (usually only a couple of minutes) the one who antagonizes leaves not giving any further thought to the confrontation, but you are left with conviction and a sense of personal failure that lingers with you the rest of the day. What's even worse, sometimes the confrontation can cause such an eruption from you it creates a situation wherein you even begin to doubt your walk with the Lord. This has happened to me on several occasions over the last few years. On more than one occasion I actually contemplated calling the pastor to tell him this Christian walk just isn't for me anymore. By the grace of God, I've never made that call and never made those comments to my pastor.

I'm unsure at times if it's just my pride or if it's the leading of the Holy Spirit that keeps me from throwing in the towel when I experience such failure in my walk with the Lord. I've always been a guy driven to finish what I start, so that probably has a lot to do with it since I really hate feeling like a failure. However, I know the Holy Spirit has started something in me He is committed to finishing, so I am confident it's more about Him giving me strength to continue than me not wanting to quit. Thank You, Jesus!

James 3:2 says that 'Indeed, we all make many mistakes. For if we could control our tongues, we would be perfect and could also control ourselves in every other way.'

Every one of us who have a desire to faithfully serve and walk with the Lord are going to fail from time to time. What you do when you fail is what will determine your future and your walk with the Lord. Many become prisoners to their weaknesses and never know the joy or freedom of being lifted out of failure by the grace, mercy and power of the Lord. The Lord is teaching me to listen for His voice when I am doing good in my walk with Him, but even more so when I fail. Just last Sunday while worshipping in church the Lord reminded me of the first time, I heard His voice. It was just the second time I had visited my church and my life at the time was in turmoil and trouble. But then I heard the Lord speak to me! Thinking back on that time so many years ago brought a smile to my face during the worship service. The praise team probably thought I was really getting into the worship, but in that moment, I was filled with joy as I remembered everything, He spoke to my heart years earlier.

Failure is inevitable and invades every area of our lives. If you are presently suffering a failure in your life, then stop and listen for the Voice of the Lord. He is closer than you might believe and if you will put your faith and trust in Him, then He will lift you out of your troubles and set your feet back on solid ground.

My dear Heavenly Father, I know I am weak and prone to failure. Without You in my life I would never know victory, but standing with You I can move mountains. Thank You for continuing to speak to my heart in that 'still small Voice'. Thank You for Your love and compassion faithfully poured out in my life day after day. Thank You for Your faithfulness, mercy and continual strength You give me through Your blessed Holy Spirit in Jesus' name. Thank You for Your presence and for enlightening my eyes to see and understand Your Word. Thank You for all You have done and for all You are doing in my life moment by moment. Thank You, Lord! In Jesus' name I pray!

Chapter Sixteen
Battle

1 John 5:19 We know that we are children of God and that the world around us is under the control of the evil one.

Hebrews 10:29 Just think how much worse the punishment will be for those who have trampled on the Son of God, and have treated the blood of the covenant, which made us holy, as if it were common and unholy, and have insulted and disdained the Holy Spirit Who brings God's mercy to us.

This chapter forces me to soberly consider the battles past and present in my own life and take personal responsibility and care to daily work out my own salvation. When I surrendered my life to Christ in 2011, I began a personal walk with Him that honestly, I knew nothing about whatsoever at the time. Even though I was raised in a loving home with parents who taught me how to know the difference between right and wrong, going to church and living a life for the Lord was not a part of our family routine. Now that I am truly 'born-again' I clearly understand being taught the difference between right and wrong, as important and foundational as that is, is still not enough. Learning the difference between right and wrong is only the beginning.

Becoming a new 'born-again' child of God is in many ways just like a baby being born into the world. There is an innocence that is precious and beautiful as the newborn child is 100% dependent upon the parents to do everything for them. However, as the child grows and matures there comes a 'day' when they begin to clearly understand the right way and the wrong way to act. From that 'day' onward the beautiful and precious moments are continuously interrupted by 'battles' that occur more and more frequently as the child willfully chooses to test the parent's moral boundaries by doing what they know is wrong. This 'challenging' must be met with strong and deliberate discipline if the 'battles' are to ever become crucial learning times teaching the child there will always be consequences for willfully choosing to disobey their loving boundaries of authority.

Fast forward to the child becoming an adult, and we see the 'battles' intensifying and becoming more severe as we take on the responsibilities of family, home, work, church, finance, health, etc. For the Christian and non-Christian alike, how we deal with these all-inclusive 'battles' is what ultimately defines us. For the Christian, how we live each day in a ever-growing non-Christian world determines whether we are live as overcomers in Christ or victims to all our circumstances (battles). In short, the 'battles' are either a well-designed (by the Lord) launchpad for victory or a platform for continual complaining resulting in a defeated lifestyle. Thankfully, I can attest that for everyone who trusts in and yields to the disciplines of our loving Father, the result is a life of blessing, peace and victory.

Far too long I ignorantly lived the way multitudes are living today, knowing the difference between right and wrong, knowing what was basically moral and immoral and trying to live a good life being nice enough to those around me. What I didn't know was that kind of effort and life is never enough to gain any favor with the God I now lovingly serve. He doesn't require me to do my best. He requires me to give my heart, trust and dependence to Christ as my Savior and allow Christ to live His life, His BEST through me. Wow! That's a lot more than just knowing the difference between right and wrong. Even still, I know I'm not where I need or long to be in my personal walk with Christ today. Thankfully, Jesus sent the Holy Spirit to work on me, in me and through me until I become like Christ in all my conduct and actions. Lord, complete Your work in and through my life!

When I made the decision to retire in 2016 it was my hope the days ahead would be defined by a stronger, more consistent walk with the Lord. I envisioned spending more and more time studying His Word, praying, witnessing and growing in the grace and knowledge of my Lord and Savior, Jesus Christ. Has that happened? Have I put Him first in my daily routine, or have I allowed other less important things to usurp my time, energy, finances and creativity? When I was working for the city of Houston, I always carried a briefcase which included a Bible, a separate book about Christ (by authors such as A.W. Tozer, Andrew Murray, C.S.

Lewis) and a notepad to write down anything the Holy Spirit spoke to my heart throughout each day. Am I showing that same kind of resolve, readiness and determination now that I'm retired? To be honest I'm tired of falling short over and over in the season I thought I would be winning battle after battle. Where do I draw the line in the sand and once for all take a stand refusing to lose any more 'battles'? How many more failures will it take before I insist on a radical change of direction and get back on track with my Heavenly Father and Savior Who loves and mercifully accepts me for who and what I am? When will I trust His promises and willingly choose to do what He has shown me is right all the time?

1 Corinthians 10:13 The temptations in your life are no different from what others experience. And God is faithful. He will not allow the temptation to be more than you can stand. When you are tempted, He will show you a way out so that you can endure.

Every man, woman and child God has ever created has been given a free will to choose between right and wrong, good and evil, God or this world. He gave us a free will that we might freely choose to accept Him, follow Him, love Him, worship Him and obey Him. For all those who choose to accept and yield to our triune Lord (Father, Son and Holy Spirit) there is the promise of continual victory and dominance over our old, sinful way of living and an abundant life in His presence. The only thing is, YOU HAVE TO CHOOSE, and you have to choose every day. That's because every day you wake up you will be confronted by new 'battles' that you didn't see coming. Sometimes I get so tired of the continual 'battles' I'm left thinking the only possible reason for it all is I'm obviously doing something terribly wrong. Then I remember the above verse and start to realize the Lord is using the 'battles' to make me more like Christ and less like what I once was. That thought shatters my original idea that living the Christian life would be much easier than living in sin and ignorance.

I'm really working on changing my attitude to where I don't wake up anymore immediately thinking the day is going to be a burden and reluctantly get out of bed already complaining and whining about the 'battles' I'm going to face. Instead, as a child of God I am determined to approach every day for the rest of my life as an opportunity to worship and thank God for giving me another opportunity to live my life for Him and His glory! I'm going to rise up each day with an attitude of gratitude hoping that will be the day I get the great honor to lead someone else to Christ. As a matter of fact, when I get up in the morning and my back is aching, something somewhere on my body is out of joint, and there is pain just putting my feet on the floor, that's going to be my platform for praise. Instead of moaning and groaning I'm going to open my mouth in thankfulness to my Lord and Savior for giving me another day on this earth to be with those I love (and who love me) and worship my faithful God with all my heart, soul, mind and strength.

Wow, that feels good just saying that I'm going to live my life that way from now on, but DOING IT over and over, day after day is where the true 'battle' rages. I'm going to be joyful, but also sober-minded knowing each day I will be tempted to fall back into anger, depression, unforgiveness and anxiety. As I feel those enemies encroaching on my mind and heart, I know all I need to do is lay them at the foot of the cross where Jesus, my Savior, already defeated them. In the shadow of the Cross of Calvary no weapon formed against me can prosper! Thank You, Jesus!

My dear Heavenly Father, may this be the 'day' I once and for all allow You to turn my life around. Through Your help, guidance, protection and power I can walk with a clear mind, a clean heart and live the rest of my life completely for You. I pray on those difficult and even dark days that I will not lose sight of You as my LIGHT to lead and guide me to certain safety and victory. Oh, how I pray that every opportunity You give me to stomp out sin I will be found courageous and expectant, rather than hesitant and unstable. Help me to grow in Your grace and knowledge that I might know Your will in every situation and circumstance thereby bringing You glory and honor by making the right choices. May I become all You have created me to be for Your glory and praise in the earth. May I be counted as a faithful warrior of Jesus Christ unafraid to face whatever giants might be

Chapter Seventeen
Soul

Matthew 10:28 *Don't be afraid of those who want to kill your body. They cannot touch your soul. Fear only God, who can destroy both soul and body in hell.*

What is a 'soul'? Webster's Dictionary defines is as: the spiritual, rational, and immortal part in man; that part of man which enables him to think, and which renders him a subject of moral government; sometimes, in distinction from the higher nature, or spirit, of man, the so-called animal soul, that is, the seat of life, the sensitive affections and phantasy, exclusive of the voluntary and rational power; sometimes in distinction from the mind, the moral and emotional part of man's nature, the seat of feeling, in distinction from intellect; sometimes, the intellect only; the understanding; the seat of knowledge, as distinguished from feeling. In a more general sense, 'an animating, separable, surviving entity, the vehicle of individual personal existence'.

The eyes of our souls only then begin to see, when our bodily eyes are closing, the seat of real life or vitality, the source of action, the animating or essential part. Thou sun of this great world both eye and soul. The leader, the inspirer, the moving spirit, the heart as the soul of an enterprise; an able general is the soul of his army. He is the very soul of bounty! Energy, courage, spirit, fervor, affection or any other noble manifestation of the heart of moral nature; inherent power or goodness; a human being; a person a familiar appellation, usually with a qualifying epithet, as 'poor soul'; God forbid so many simple souls should perish by the sword!

One Sunday after church my only grandson at the time, Jake, wanted to ride home with Pawpaw. On the way home we drove with the windows down listening to music being played on the local Christian radio station. What a joy it was listening to this little voice in the back seat singing along with the songs being played. At some point during our drive home the song, 'Soul on Fire', came on. This is a song with a faster, upbeat tempo, so I turned the radio up so we could both rock out to Jesus as we drove along with the windows down. Watching and hearing my grandson belting out the song (as best he could) loud and clear put a smile on my face that stretched from side to side on my truck. But then all of a sudden, he just stopped and went completely silent in the back seat. I quickly looked in the rearview mirror to see what was going on and noticed him sitting there quietly with a look of bewilderment on his face. I turned the music down then asked, 'Hey bud, what's wrong?' He broke his silence with a question: 'Pawpaw, what's a soul?' Realizing he was only six years old I tried to answer his question in a way I thought would better help a little boy understand. 'Well, buddy, a soul is something God puts deep inside everyone's body, deep down inside where your heart is. It's a lot like when you're outside and the sun is shining so bright you can see your shadow on the ground behind you. 'Do you understand what Pawpaw is saying?' In a second he simply responded (just like a six-year-old), 'Oh, ok.' Thankfully we were stopped in traffic when he fired back another obvious question for a six-year-old boy: 'Pawpaw, why would that man want his soul to be on fire?' I immediately erupted in spontaneous laughter before gathering myself enough to respond to his second question. 'Buddy, what the singer is saying is he really wants the Lord to fill his heart with a love for Him that is like a huge fire that can't be put out. That means he is asking the Lord to fill his heart with a love for the Bible and for Jesus. He's not asking that his heart be physically on fire, but that the Lord would fill his heart with the warmth of His presence so his thoughts and feelings would always be on the Lord, and that every step he takes every single day would be guided by the Lord.' After I answered his second question I waited quietly (and to be honest a little nervously) for his response. After only a few seconds he replied, 'Oh, ok. I understand. He just wants to love God.' With a sigh of relief, I replied, 'Right! You got it.' And just as quickly as that entire dialogue started it was over as the next song came on and he moved on singing to the new song on the radio. Although I have no remembrance of what the next song was, I will never forget that afternoon with my six-year-old grandson and the amazing conversation we had together.

The lesson I've learned and continue to be challenged by through this story is simple: If I struggle to find the words to explain to a six-year-old what a soul really is, then how am I going to explain to any adult I meet the eternal importance of their soul being on fire for the Lord? Thankfully, the wisdom and knowledge I still lack are readily available from our loving and gracious Lord to all who simply ask, if they ask with a sincere and humble heart. As we encounter people in the world, no matter how difficult the questions might be they ask of us, we can be assured our merciful God will give us the wisdom, grace and compassion we lack and strengthen us when we are weak.

So, in closing I must ask, 'Who is it that really has your soul? Do you really know for certain where your soul will be in eternity?'

My dear heavenly Father, thank You for all the people You have placed in my life to help guide to be secure in my walk with You and my place in Your Kingdom. As You lead me forward strengthen my foundation that I might always stand on the Rock that is Your Son, Jesus Christ. By Your grace, guidance and anointing help me to be Your witness that I might see lost and broken souls come into Your Kingdom. Thank You, thank You, thank You for all You continually do for me and my family moment by moment, day after day. In gratitude for all You have made possible and all You have done take my life and let it be a continual reflection of Your Light, Your Life, Your Word and Your Son. Flow through my soul like a mighty rushing river. In Jesus' name, I pray. Amen.

Chapter Eighteen
Underestimated!

Philippians 2:3,4 *Don't be selfish. Don't try to impress others. Be humble, thinking of others as better than yourselves. Don't look out only for your own interests, but take an interest in others, too.*

Have you ever underestimated someone after just meeting them? How many times have you found yourself in a situation wherein you were left scratching your head wondering what just happened? Now turn that around and let me ask, 'Has anyone ever underestimated you after first meeting you? Or, have you ever had anyone try to embarrass or intimidate you in front of others after meeting you? I think we can all say 'Yes' to these questions, can't we?

When I was fourteen years old my family and I moved from our little town in Iowa to a part of the country that seemed like another world to me at the time. That place was southern Arkansas. Having lived all fourteen years of my life in Iowa meant I had never attended school anywhere but in the small town where I grew up. Needless to say, it was a dramatic change for a teenager from the Midwest. Upon arriving in Arkansas, we moved into a community near Millwood Country Club which was a public facility with a nice pool, a feature I especially liked. Thankfully it didn't take long to make some new friends. One weekend a couple of my new friends and I decided to head over to the club to check out the pool and possibly go for a swim. The pool was a good size with a single diving board on the deep end as well as clearly marked black stripes on the floor of the pool. I had spent six years on the swim team in my former town, so I immediately assumed this pool, which was also 25 meters in length, had been set up for swim meets. My two friends and I quickly settled in and were having an easy, uneventful day until a college student showed up and started strutting about like a peacock bragging to everyone that he was on the Arkansas Razorback's swim team. None of that would have bothered me at all, but this guy kept going on and on becoming more and more obnoxious and rude in the process until it was ruining everyone's afternoon. If that wasn't enough, he then started challenging anyone there to race against him so he could show off his athletic prowess. There were several other guys at the pool who were all older than me, but none of them would accept this guy's continual challenges. Finally, I got so aggravated with this guy I walked up and accepted the challenge which was a 25-meter sprint, or one length of the pool. I figured there was nothing to lose, and maybe my accepting his challenge would shut this guy up for a while. Anyway, I have always loved a challenge and at that moment thought it would be fun to race this cocky guy. Since it was a public pool there were lifeguards on duty who had been listening to this guy from the start. When I accepted the challenge, the lifeguards stepped in and said they would call the start of the race and announce the winner at the other end of the pool. While the lifeguards were clearing the pool I had a brief moment to speak to the college guy. The only thing he said to me was he was surprised I had accepted his challenge. The lifeguard at the starting point then had us both line up at the edge of the pool. I curled my toes down over the edge for maximum push off and got in my normal starting position waiting for the whistle to blow and the race to start. 'On your marks! Set! Go!' I exploded out into the water before the lifeguard's voice had quit ringing out the start signal. As we were swimming, I could see I was a little ahead at the halfway point. Seconds later as we touched the other side of the pool and raised our heads out of the water, I was surprised to hear the lifeguard calling the collegiate swimmer the winner. As we were exiting the water the collegiate swimmer spoke to me again saying, 'You almost got me. I really underestimated you'. I simply thanked him for letting a young teenager compete against a collegiate swimmer.

That memorable day was a time a collegiate swimmer did something we all do too many times, let his pride and ego get out of hand and almost cause him a lifetime of embarrassment. Had I beaten him that day he would have lost in more ways than just in the pool. Even though he was braggadocious to the point of being obnoxious, his biggest mistake that day was casually underestimating his opponent. I'm sure we can all admit to having underestimated our opposition or enemies at some point in our past. However, our biggest mistake as children of God is constantly underestimating the Lord, and His grace, love, forgiveness, and power.

I am fairly confident most of you reading this have already made the all-important decision to turn your life over to Jesus confessing Him as your Lord and receiving Him as your only Hope of Salvation. Hallelujah! Now that you've made that eternally crucial decision, do you still hang on to your daily problems and spend hours and hours worrying about the very things you've already surrendered to your Lord? If so, then you, like me, are underestimating your Savior and Lord not taking into account or trusting in His promises to protect and provide for you all the days of your life.

I am also fairly confident some of you reading this have never made the life-changing decision to surrender your life and heart to Jesus, plead for His unconditional mercy and repent of your sins, and receive Him as your Lord and Savior. You, too, have grossly underestimated His love for you, and His desire to have you as His loving child living with Him in His eternal Kingdom forever. Oh, how He longs for you to lay down your pride and unbelief and trust in His love and purpose for your life. We all come to this valley of decision, but only a few choose wisely and call upon Jesus as their Lord and Savior. Multitudes underestimate the importance of this decision, and therefore underestimate the judgment of God who will not allow anyone in His Kingdom unless they have yielded and surrendered their lives to His Son, Jesus Christ, as their Lord, Master and Savior.

My Father in heaven, I know I have underestimated Your love and grace, and have ignorantly taken advantage of Your patience. I pray the days of my underestimating You and all You have promised are over. Oh, how I long to be more and more intimate with You, more and more trusting, more and more confident in all Your promises and Your resolve to keep those promises on my behalf. I long for You to know and sense my sincere love for You. Help me, Lord for I am weak and so easily distracted. I pray my relationship with You is so vibrant and real that others see having a loving, intimate relationship with You is not only possible, but available in that very moment. Thank You, for Your mercy, patience, love and forgiveness continually shown toward me and my family. I love You, Lord. I pray all this in Jesus' name. Amen.

Chapter Nineteen
Church

Acts 20:28-30 So guard yourselves and God's people. Feed and shepherd God's flock, His church, purchased with His own blood over which the Holy Spirit has appointed you as leaders. I know that false teachers, like vicious wolves, will come in among you after I leave, not sparing the flock. Even some men from your own group will rise up and distort the truth in order to draw a following.

The importance of finding the right church is a subject close to my heart. Although I was never raised in a home that attended church regularly, I was taught to be truthful and considerate of others that cross your path along the way giving them respect regardless of their age, race or social status. In other words, I was taught the 'golden rule' to treat others the same way I wanted them to treat me.

Well, have I met a lot of different and interesting people over the last forty years on my journey to ultimately find God and make Him the center and focus of my life's walk. Surprisingly, along the way finding that family of believers (church) who were corporately searching for the same 'walk' with the Lord that we are striving for, a place where the Bible is taught as the infallible TRUTH, a place that believes in an old-fashioned altar where people confess their sin, and a place we felt welcomed, loved, and accepted hasn't been so easy. We longed for a church where everyone could feel the presence of God and experience His loving touch on their lives. I sincerely believe had we found such a church much earlier in the journey my walk with the Lord would have become much stronger and more consistent much earlier than it has in my walk with the Lord. Sadly, what we have found to be common each time we searched for a family of believers we could call home was a group of people who gathered more out of convenience than anything else. For us church will always be about devotion and commitment, and being committed to church is one of the most important decisions any family or person will ever make. I look at it like this: when you purchase a new vehicle, you expect that vehicle to be dependable for at least three years, and hopefully many more before having to consider trading it in on another new vehicle. Of course, there are those times unfortunate and unexpected things happen such as accidents or major mechanical failures which forces you to get another vehicle, but those times thankfully rarely happen. Similarly, when most people purchase a home, they do so with the expectation of living in it for many years. I know for us, when we purchased our home, we did so with the thought this would be our 'forever' home. What I'm getting at is even when you believe you've found a rock-solid church family; you still need to understand that sometimes even a church can experience breakdowns or spiritual wrecks that demand you make the difficult decision to find another church family. Thousands of churches in America that once stood for the Gospel of Jesus Christ are now turning a blind eye to flagrant sin and catering to people's desires rather than remaining committed to the infallible TRUTH of the Word of God. I've experienced this firsthand in my own family. The wonderful family I married into had been attending the same church for more than fifty years and were foundational building blocks in this particular church's history. It was in this church they became relentless in their love and pursuit of the Lord. It was in this church my wife's family found God's purpose and call for their lives, and then experience the great joy of seeing that call and purpose being fulfilled year after year. Consequently, the church became the center of their lives as they spent more time serving in church than doing anything else in their lives. After more than five decades of faithful service in their church my father-in-law passed away. His funeral was truly a celebration service held at the church they had so faithfully served from the 1960's. Soon after his death my mother-in-law planned out every detail of her funeral service complete with music, poems, scriptures and her favorite hymn she wanted sung when the time came for her life to be remembered and celebrated. She even chose which pastor she wanted to lead her service, a pastor she had personally known, loved in the Lord and served for decades. It wasn't long before her health began failing, then at the age of 86 she gloriously went on to be with the Lord. Immediately following her death, my wife called the church her parents had loved and served for most of her life letting them know of her passing so the church could move forward with the necessary plans for her funeral at the church. Thankfully, the same pastors my mother and father-in-law had loved and served for most of their adult lives were still leading the church at the time of my mother in law's death. When my wife called the church, she, of course, first spoke to the church receptionist. Upon hearing of my mother in law's passing the receptionist informed my wife she had better get a 'back up plan' in place as part of the church was under construction. My wife simply requested for the receptionist to ask one of the younger pastors (a young man my wife had grown up with in the church who was also the son of the Senior pastor) to give her a call so they could work out the details of her mother's funeral together. Instead of receiving a call from the younger pastor, she received a call from the church's funeral director (yes, this is a large church and has a funeral director on staff). This individual promptly informed us that NOT only was the main church sanctuary unavailable, but none of the three other satellite church locations were available either to hold the services. My wife then asked the funeral director at the church to please have one of the head pastors call her, men she had personally known most of her adult life. After a week she was still waiting for any call from any of the pastors at the church her parents had faithfully and sacrificially served for so long. The only recourse my wife had at that point was to contact a local funeral home and schedule her mother's service. Thankfully, one of the younger pastors at the church agreed to come and officiate the service at the funeral home.

The punch line to this story is simple, people come and go in our lives, church facilities come and go in our lives, but only one thing remains constant, and that is the love and commitment the Lord has for us all. My suggestion to any of you searching for a church home is first to pray. Ask the Lord to lead you to a family of believers who first and foremost love Jesus, but to pastors who value the people far more than they value the buildings where the people gather. Lastly, once the Lord has led you to a body of believers who are like-minded and passionate to worship and serve the Lord, guard your mind and maintain a servant's heart no matter who or what changes around you. And whatever you do, do it for the Lord and His glory!

My dear Father God, thank You for being so patient with me throughout all these years. Thank You for never giving up on me during all the years I ignorantly and selfishly wandered about pursuing my own plan. Thank You for graciously allowing me the privilege and opportunity to search for the TRUTH about Who You are and what You created me to accomplish for You. Thank You, my Father, for guiding and directing my path, and when I've wandered from that path, for bringing me back to the straight and narrow path You've designed for me to walk. Thank You for the church You led me and my family to become part of these past many years. I sincerely look forward to better and greater days ahead as You lead me onward and upward in this glorious walk of faith. I love You, Lord! Amen!

Made in the USA
Columbia, SC
20 October 2021